Introduction to Database Systems

By Darrell Hajek and Flor Narciso

Darrell Hajek received his PhD. In mathematics in 1971 from the University of Florida. He was immediately hired by the University of Puerto Rico at Mayaguez (RUM) and worked there until his retirement in June 2019, teaching mathematics and computer science (10 years as department chair.) He has approximately 50 mathematics publications in refereed journals as well as several books in computer graphics, computer literacy and fiction/fantasy.

Flor Narciso received her MS in Informatics in 1988 from the Universidad Politécnica de Madrid, and her Ph.D. in Computer Science and Engineering in 1999 from the University of South Florida. She was a professor at the University of the Andes in Venezuela for 31 years, and in 2014 was hired by the University of Puerto Rico at Mayaguez (RUM), where she has been teaching computer science. She has participated in congresses, conferences and colloquiums, and has publications in congresses, conferences, scientific journals and chapters in books. Currently, she is the Acting Associate Director of the Department of Mathematical Sciences of the RUM.

Books Co-authored by Darrell Hajek and Cesar Herrera

Introduction to Computers

Introduction to Computers 2018 Edition

Introduction to Computers 2019 Edition

Principles of Operating Systems

Principles of Operating Systems 2019 Edition

Co-authored by Darrell Hajek, Cesar Herrera and Flor Narciso

Principles of Operating Systems 2020 Edition

Other books by Darrell Hajek

Introduction to Computer Graphics

Introduction to Computer Graphics 2018 Edition

Introduction to Computer Graphics 2019 Edition

Introduction to Office Productivity Software: Word-Excel-PowerPoint

Introduction to Office Software: Word-Excel-PowerPoint-Paint

Introduction to LibreOffice Productivity Software: Writer-Calc-Impress

Winning at Lotto

Life and Times of Harry Wolf

Life and Times of Harry Wolf Expanded Edition

Life and Times of Harry Wolf Augmented Expanded Edition

Life and Times of Harry Wolf 2018 Edition

Life and Times of Harry Wolf 2019 Edition

Life and Times of Harry Wolf 2020 Edition

Preface:

We have noticed that very few students in our database courses were purchasing the assigned text, probably because they felt it was too expensive. Several (it is rumored) had resorted to downloading (illegal) digital copies.

Not wanting to motivate illegal activities on the part of our students, we have set out to produce a more reasonably priced alternative.

We have tried to include all the material necessary for a basic course in database systems, but, in order to keep a low price for our students, we have attempted to keep the content to ONLY what would be necessary for such a course. We fully expect that many will disagree with the choices we have made, both in what we have included and (probably even more) in what we have failed to include. We will revisit these decisions when we prepare future editions. Suggestions and recommendations are welcome.

We will be creating a set of supplementary PowerPoint files for the text as well as a testbank. We will be happy to make both available to any teacher who chooses to adopt the book as assigned text for a course.

You are welcome to contact us at:

darrell.hajek@upr.edu

flor.narciso@upr.edu

Contents

Chapter 1 Introduction 1

    1.1 Why do we need database systems 1

    1.2 Database system components 1

    1.3 Databases in our Lives 2

    1.4 Functions of a DBMS 3

    1.5 DBMS Development 4

    1.6 Database Sizes 5

    1.7 Data Types 6

    1.8 Types of Database Systems 6

    1.9 Hardware Components 6

    1.10 Database Users 6

Chapter 2 Data Models 9

    2.1 Concepts involved in Data Models 9

    2.2 Data Models Currently Used 10

    2.3 The Relational Model 10

    2.4 The Semistructured Model 11

    2.5 Other Data Models 12

    2.6 Comparing Modelling Approaches 13

    2.7 Basics of the Relational Model 13

    2.8 Defining a Relation Schema in SQL 18

    2.9 Example System: 28

    2.10 Example Instance of Database with Above Example Schema 30

Chapter 3 Algebraic Query Language 33

    3.1 Why Do We Need a *"Query Language"* 33

    3.2 Relational Algebra and Database Queries 33

    3.3 Algebraic Query Language 43

Chapter 4 Design Theory for Relational Databases: Functional Dependencies 51

    4.1 Functional Dependencies 51

4.2 Rules About Functional Dependencies 54

4.3 Design of Relational Databases 59

Chapter 5 Design Theory for Relational Databases: Normal Forms 63

5.1 Design of Relational Databases Boyce-Codd Normal Form 63

5.2 Third Normal Form 69

5.3 Multivalued Dependencies 71

5.4 Fourth Normal Form 74

5.5 Why the Chase Works, FD's and MVD's 77

Chapter 6 High Level Database Models – E/R Diagrams 79

6.1 High Level Design 79

6.2 The Entity/Relationship Model 80

6.3 Design Principles 84

6.4 Constraints in the E/R Model 86

6.5 Weak Entity Sets in the E/R Model 88

6.6 From E/R Diagrams to Relational Designs 89

Chapter 7 High Level Database Models - UML 99

7.1 UML Classes 99

7.2 UML Associations 99

7.3 Subclasses in UML 101

7.4 Aggregations and Compositions 102

7.5 From UML Diagrams to Relations 103

7.6 The UML Analog of Weak Entity Sets 105

7.7 Object Definition Language 106

Chapter 8 Algebraic and Logical Query Languages 117

8.1 Relational Operations on Bags 117

8.2 Extended Relational Operations 120

9.0 The Database Language SQL 128

9.1 Simple Queries in SQL 128

9.2 Selection in SQL 131

9.3 Dates and Times in SQL.. 132

9.4 Null Values in SQL and Comparisons involving Null 133

9.5 The Truth Value UNKNOWN 134

9.6 Ordering the Output 135

9.7 Queries Involving More than One Relation... 135

9.8 Union, Intersection and Difference of Queries 138

9.9 Subqueries in SQL 139

9.10 SQL Join Operations 142

9.11 SQL Relation Operations 144

9.12 SQL Database Modifications 147

9.13 SQL Transactions... 149

10.0 Constraints.. 155

10.1 Keys and Foreign Keys 155

10.2 Constraints on Attributes and Tuples 159

10.3 Modification of Constraints 160

10.4 Assertions 161

11.0 Views and Indexes 164

11.1 Views 164

11.2 ModifyingViews 165

11.3 Materialized Views 167

11.4 Indexes in SQL.. 168

11.5 Security in SQL 170

11.5.1 Authorization ID's 170

11.5.2 Privileges.. 171

11.5.3 Granting Privileges... 171

11.5.4 Revoking Privileges 172

Answers to Odd Numbered Questions 176

Introduction

1.1 Why do we need database systems

Information and communication are becoming larger and larger factors in all of our lives. The quantities of information are becoming larger and larger and its interrelationships are becoming more and more complex. This has motivated the development of elaborate systems for dealing with this information: its storage, its utilization, means for both accessing it efficiently and protecting it.

The systems that have been developed for dealing with these large complex collections of information are called *Database Systems*.

a database system is a computerized record-keeping system – A system whose purpose is to store information and allow users to access that information and update it.

Such a system involves 4 major components:
– Data
– Hardware
– Software
– Users

1.2 Database system components

A complete database system will involve a database (having data stored in a format defined by a *database management system*) a user interface and an interface between the user interface and the database (often a network server.)

1.2.1 Database Management System (DBMS)

A DBMS is a program (or collection of programs) designed to manipulate, access and, in general, control data stored in a *database*.

A DBMS will typically be controlled by commands (and programs) written in SQL, a language which was originally designed by IBM for its proprietary DBMS (named System R), but which has since been adopted (with minor variations) by virtually all designers of DBMS software. Standards for SQL have been published by both ANSI and ISO.

The most widely used commercial DBMS software is by Oracle.

MYSQL is a widely used free open source DBMS.

1.2.1.1 SQL

Examples of SQL commands include: SELECT, INSERT, DELETE, UPDATE

In SQL, individual data files are called *tables*

(SQL is designed primarily for what are referred to as *relational* databases)

An individual *record* in such a data file is called a *row* of the table

The columns in the tables are identified as *fields*

1

Introduction

1.2.2 User Interface

The use of direct interfaces for communication between user and database is especially common for small local systems (address books on smartphones for example) but all major DBMS's provide direct user interfaces[1].

Many applications require remote user access and remote access typically utilizes the Internet for communication between database programs and remote users. These remote users use the browsers on their personal computers. Browser displays on users' computers are controlled by HTML and have subprograms in JavaScript for dynamic content.

1.2.3 Network Server

An HTML program running on a browser will typically be communicating with a network server. For database applications the network server would function as an interface between the user and a DBMS system, (quite possibly on still another computer.) The server interface program might be written in just about any programming language, but PHP is probably the most common.

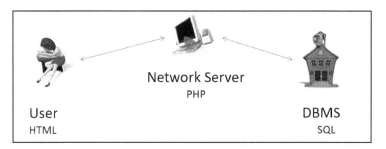

1.3 Databases in our Lives

Databases have become pervasive in our lives

- Even our smart phones have built in database systems and every time one of us turns on our cellphone, we are accessing a database.
- Whenever we visit a major Web site (Google, Yahoo, Amazon, …) there will be a database to provide whatever information we might request (and record any purchases we might make.)
- Corporations (and many individuals) maintain business records (and other types of data as well) in databases.
- Databases are found at the core of many scientific investigations, representing and helping to organize data gathered by researchers in many (most, if not all) areas.

---

[1] Systems administrators typically require direct access.

2

Introduction

1.4 Functions of a DBMS

The power of databases comes from a body of knowledge and technology that has developed over several decades and is embodied in specialized software systems which are called *database management systems* (DBMS's), as indicated above.

A DBMS serves as a layer of software to provide an interface between the user and the physical representations of the data in the database.
- Requests for access to the database are processed by the DBMS.
- Facilities for adding, removing and updating data are provided by the DBMS.
- The DBMS makes it unnecessary for the users to concern themselves with the details of data representation or operation implementation.

A DBMS provides a powerful tool for creating and managing large amounts of data efficiently and allowing it to persist safely over long periods of time. These systems are among the most complex types of software available.

Technically, the term *database* only refers to a collection of *information* (a collection that persists over a period of time, often many years.) In common parlance, however, the term database tends to refer to any collection of data that is managed by a DBMS.

A DBMS is expected to:

1. Allow users to create new databases and specify their schemas (logical structures of the data) using a specialized data-definition language.

2. Give users the ability to query the data and modify the data using an appropriate language (often called a *query[2] language* or *data-manipulation language.*)

3. Support the storage of large amounts of data over a long period of time and allow efficient access to the data for purposes of querying and/or modifying the data. (Data stored in a database must be *persistent*.)

   a. After having been stored in the database, it remains/persists in the system, available for retrieval/modification until another operation deletes or changes it

      i. This differs from other types of data, such as input data and output data, which tend to be *transient* in nature

   b. Persistent data can only be removed from the database by an explicit operation of the DBMS, and not as the side effect of an operation not specifically designed to remove it.

4. Support the recovery of databases following errors and/or failures and protect against partial operations.

5. Control access to data from many users at once without allowing unexpected interactions.

---

[2]   A *query* is a question about the data

Introduction

The first important DBMS's were developed to support systems in which data was composed of many small items and in which many queries and/or modifications were made:

- Banking systems which must maintain accounts and must insure that system failures do not make money appear or disappear.

- Airline reservation systems which must accept large numbers of small actions by customers, often concurrently.

- Corporate record keeping for maintaining and tracking such things as employment and tax records, inventories, and sales records.

1.5.1 Earliest DBMS Models

There were several early DBMS models used for describing the structure of database information. Prominent among them:

- The hierarchical (tree based) model

- The network (graph based) model

These early models did not support high level query languages. With these early systems each database had its own querying system and a user would have to learn a new system when beginning to work with each new database.

1.5.2 Relational Databases

In 1970, Ted Codd suggested that:

- Database systems should present the user with a view of data organized as *tables* (which he chose to call **relations**.)

- The programmers of such a *relational* system should not need to be concerned with the storage structure.

- In such a *relational* system queries can be expressed in a high level language.

- The use of such a system would result in greatly increased efficiency of database programmers

The most important of the high level languages that were developed based on this relational model was SQL (structured query language.) By the 1990's the relational model, using SQL, had become the norm for database systems.

The field continues to evolve, however, and object-oriented features are being integrated into the relational model

Introduction

1.5.3 Trends in DBMS Development

Originally DBMS's were large expensive programs running only on large expensive machines.

- At that time, storage space for quantities of data that would require a DBMS was only available on such machines.

Later, smaller (personal) computers began appearing with greater storage capacities Then smaller DBMS's were developed that would run on these smaller computers.

Another modern trend is the use of XML documents

- Large collections of small XML tagged documents can serve as a database
- Methods of querying and manipulating XML documents are quite different from those used in relational databases.

1.6 Database Sizes

Many systems today must deal with larger collections of data than were ever *conceived* of earlier (in the 1960's and 1970's.)

Corporate databases routinely store terabytes (10^{12}bytes = 1000 GB) of data.

Many databases store *petabytes* (10^{15} bytes = 1000 TB) of data:

Google holds petabytes of data obtained from Webcrawls.

Communications satellites send down petabytes of information

Graphic images typically require several thousand or more bytes (usually more and often MUCH more) and repositories such as Flickr routinely store millions of graphic images (and, of course, they must support *searches* of these images.)

An hour of video requires at least a gigabyte of data and sites such as YouTube hold hundreds of thousands (even millions) of movies (and make them easily available.)

Peer to peer file sharing systems, such as BitTorrent and Gnutella, form truly enormous databases.

1.6.1 Data Integration

One of the major types of problems that has developed for the design and maintenance of databases is that of information *integration*.

The joining/combining of information contained in many different databases into a single whole database.

Large companies have many divisions, each of which has its own database

When one company acquires another, the company acquired will have had its own legacy data and its legacy software might be quite different than that of the acquiring company.

With increasing frequency, it has become necessary to build structures on top of existing databases with the goal of integrating the information distributed among them.

One popular approach to large scale information integration is the creation of *data warehouses*

- Information from many different databases is copied periodically to a central database from where it is redistributed where and when needed.

Another approach is the implementation of a mediator or "middleware" whose function is to support an integrated model of the data in the various databases, and translating information from this model into those used by the various databases in the system.

Introduction

1.7 Data Types

The most common types of data that will be stored in the column entries of a database table are numerical and character strings, but most DBMS systems also support other data types as well:
Dates and times
Images
Audio and video
Many others …

1.8 Types of Database Systems

Database systems are available on many kinds of computing systems ranging from small handheld personal computers up to clusters of mainframes.

The facilities provided by a given system will be determined (at least to an extent) by the size and power of the underlying machine(s)

DB systems on large machines tend to be multi-user systems, while those on smaller machines are often single user systems.

A single-user system is one in which only one user can access the database at any given time.

A multi-user system is one in which many users can access the database simultaneously (Although, typically, each user behaves as if he were working on a single user system.)

The data in a database will normally be both *integrated* and *shared:*

- By *integrated*, we mean that the data will be stored in several distinct files, but that all (or at least *most*) redundancies will have been eliminated.

- By *shared*, we mean that the data can be accessed by many different users:

Any given user will probably only be concerned with a portion of the database, but, in fact, the portions accessed by different users will often overlap.

1.9 Hardware Components

The hardware components consist of:

- Secondary storage and associated I/O devices, device controllers, etc.
Storage is typically on magnetic disks
Used for data storage and retrieval

- Processor(s) and associated main memory
Used to support the execution of database system software

1.10 Database Users

There are three classes of users:

- Application programmers:
Application programmers are responsible for writing interface programs in a high level language (typically SQL.)

- End users
Access the database by means of interface programs (written by application programmers) or using built-in interfaces

- Database administrators
Database administrators (DBAs) use specialized software to store and organize data, such as financial information and customer shipping records.
They make sure that data are available to users and secure from unauthorized access

Introduction

1.11 Chapter 1 Questions

1.11.1 TRUE/FALSE

1.11.1.1 In common parlance, the term database tends to refer to a collection of data that is managed by a DBMS

1.11.1.2 Data stored in a database must be *transient*

1.11.1.3 Early DBMS's did not support high level query languages

1.11.1.4 Any given user will probably only be concerned with a portion of the database, and, the portions accessed by different users will never overlap

1.11.2 MULTIPLE CHOICE

1.11.2.1 A DBMS will typically be controlled by commands (and programs) written in _____, a language originally designed by IBM but which has since been adopted (with minor variations) by all designers of DBMS software.
a.   SQL
b.   ISO
c.   ANSI
d.   Oracle
e.   none of the above

1.11.2.2 The first important DBMS's were ones where data was composed of many small items and many queries and/or modifications were made. An example would be
a.   a banking system
b.   an airline reservation system
c.   corporate record keeping
d.   all of the above
e.   none of the above

1.11.2.3 The data in a database will normally be:
a.   *integrated* but not *shared*
b.   *shared* but not *integrated*
c.   both *integrated* and *shared*
d.   neither *integrated* nor *shared*
e.   none of the above

1.11.3 COMPLETION

1.11.3.1 A(n) _____ system is a computerized record-keeping system – A system whose purpose is to store information and allow users to update and retrieve the information

1.11.3.2 Browser displays on user computers are controlled by HTML and have subprograms in _____ for dynamic content

1.11.3.3 There were several early DBMS models used for describing the structure of database information. Prominent among them:
  – The _____ (tree based) model
  – The graph based (network) model

1.11.3.4 In 1970 , Ted Codd proposed that database systems should present the user with a view of data organized as _____

1.11.3.5 By the 1990's the _____ model had become the norm

Introduction

1.11.3.6 A popular approach to large scale information integration is the implementation of a *mediator* or "_____" whose function is to support an integrated model of the data in the various databases, and translating information from this model into those used by the various databases in the system

1.11.3.7 When we say that the data in a database is _____ we mean that the data will be stored in several distinct files, but that most redundancies will have been eliminated.

Chapter 2 Data Models

A database system involves the representation of information (data/entities) but it also involves interrelationships among the entities.

As an example: a school, must keep records of classes being offered and it must keep records of who it is that is enrolled in the school (who the students are).

(Students and classes are, of course, two very different kinds of entities and have very different kinds of characteristics.)

The school must also keep track of which students are enrolled in which classes (a relationship between students and classes.)

Clearly it is important that a database for the school include representations of the class enrollment relations as well as the data specific to the students and classes.

In order to design a system for dealing with complex data and complex interrelationships, one needs a *model* that organizes elements of the data and standardizes how they relate to one another, as well as to the properties of the real world entities they represent.

The notion of a data *model*, then, is fundamental to the study of database systems.

2.1 Concepts involved in Data Models

Some of the important concepts involved in data models are:

–*Structure* of data

–*Operations* on data

–*Constraints* on data

2.1.1 Structure of Data

The data in a data model must, of course, be represented in computer memory/storage and this representation will (must) involve data *structures* (arrays, objects, structs, …)

These data structures involved in the physical storage for elements in a data model are sometimes referred to as the *physical* data model.

Data models and database implementations typically involve structures, operations and constraints specific to database/data models and at this level, the structures are referred to as the *conceptual* model.

2.1.2 Operations on Data

In a database *data* model there will usually be only a limited set of operations that can be performed. These operations can be divided into two classifications: *queries* and *modifications*:

Queries are operations that *retrieve* information.

Modifications are operations that make *changes* in elements of the database.

Limiting the available operations, makes it possible for programmers to describe database operations at a higher level, and permits the database management system to implement these operations efficiently.

Systems with fewer limitations do not support optimization. They do not support optimization precisely because they allow the programmer to specify less than optimal algorithms.

Data Models

2.1.3 Constraints on Data

Database models usually have ways to describe limitations on the kinds of data that can be represented.

Many of these limitations (constraints) are simple and straightforward
 (data representing a number of minutes must be nonnegative and less than 60)
 (representations of numbers of inches should be less than 12)
but some constraints are extremely complex.

2.2 Data Models Currently Used

There are two important data models in wide use today: the relational model and the semistructured model.

2.2.1 The relational model

The relational model is the one used in all (current) commercial database systems.

When people talk about "*databases*" and "*database systems*" this is the one they are probably talking about.

 The concept of "relational model" has recently begun being extended to include some "object-oriented" capabilities.

2.2.2 The semistructured model

XML is the primary example of a semistructured model.

XML capabilities have also begun appearing in many database systems (generally as added features.)

2.3 The Relational Model

The *relational* model is based on *tables*.

2.3.1 The Relational Model: Structure of the data

In Figure 2-01 we have an example of a table describing classes offered at a (fictional) college. Each class would be offered by a specific department/program. It would have a specific course number, and an identifying section

Classes				
ProgramID	CourseNumber	SectionNumber	TeacherIDNumber	RoomID
BIOL	2212	020	444917012	DUP311
COMP	1001	011	744500105	TUR203
MATH	3101	122	514067723	FUN101
SCLP	4123	161	888991121	HUM202

Figure 2-01

number. It identifies the professor assigned to teach the course and the classroom where it meets.

The table shown in Figure 2-01 only has four rows (each representing a class) but one can imagine that in real life a college would offer many more than four classes, and so, a table describing all classes at the college would have many more rows than are shown here.

Adding more classes will not change the basic structure of the table. Each class has a program under which it is offered (identified using a four letter code) a course number, a section number, a teacher and a classroom where it meets.

Data Models

For a C programmer, such a table is an *array* of *structs*[3]: each row in the table an element of the array and each column corresponding to a struct field name. Such an implementation is, of course, possible but would be problematic for any but the most elementary data manipulations. Programming an application in C (or similar programming language) for such a database would require the programmer to essentially reinvent most of the components of a database management system.

2.3.2 The Relational Model: Operations on the data

The operations normally associated with the relational model[4] form the "relational algebra" for the system. These operations are:

Selection, Projection, Product, Union and Difference

These operations are, of course, all "*table* oriented".

2.3.3 The Relational Model: Constraints on the data

The data in a database is generally subject to many different constraints. What constraints would be appropriate will depend on what it is that is being represented.

Example: The table from Figure 2-01, holds information about classes being taught at a college. This college (any college) offers only limited number of programs. The entries in the "ProgramID" field, then, would be required (i.e. *constrained*) to be the identifier for one of the programs offered at the college.

An attempt to create a row representing a class of METH 1003 should almost certainly result in an error message (Since the college probably does not have a "METH" program.)

No two rows of the table should have identical values in the "Program", "Course" and "Section" fields, since two such rows would describe the same class.

2.4 The Semistructured Model

The data in a semistructured system will have a structure more like trees or graphs than that of a table or array.

XML is the principal modern example of a semistructured system.

---

[3] Other languages might use different names for these data types, but most modern languages will provide structures for these kinds of data representation.

[4] Described by E.F. Codd in 1970

Data Models

2.4.1 The Semistructured Model: XML

XML structures its data representations using hierarchically nested tagged elements. The tags define the role played by different pieces of data in much the same way as column headers in the relational model.

Figure 2-02 shows how the information from table in Figure 2-01 might be described using XML

2.4.2 The Semistructured Model: Data Operations

The operations on semistructured models generally involve following paths in the (implied) tree. Paths from an element to one or more of its nested subelements, then to subelements within those and so on.

2.4.3 The Semistructured Model: Constraints on Data

```
<Classes>
  <ClassID>
    <ProgramID>BIOL</ProgramID>
    <CourseNumber>2212</CourseNumber>
    <SectionNumber>020</SectionNumber>
    <TeacherIDNumber>444917012</TeacherIDNumber>
    <RoomID>DUP311</RoomID>
  </ClassID>
  <ClassID>
    <ProgramID>COMP</ProgramID>
    <CourseNumber>1001</CourseNumber>
    <SectionNumber>011</SectionNumber>
    <TeacherIDNumber>744500105</TeacherIDNumber>
    <RoomID>TUR203</RoomID>
  </ClassID>
  <ClassID>
    <ProgramID>MATH</ProgramID>
    <CourseNumber>3101</CourseNumber>
    <SectionNumber>122</SectionNumber>
    <TeacherIDNumber>514067723</TeacherIDNumber>
    <RoomID>FUN101</RoomID>
  </ClassID>
  <ClassID>
    <ProgramID>SCLP</ProgramID>
    <CourseNumber>4123</CourseNumber>
    <SectionNumber>161</SectionNumber>
    <TeacherIDNumber>888991121</TeacherIDNumber>
    <RoomID>HUM202</RoomID>
  </ClassID>
</Classes>
```

Figure 2-02

The constraints on data in semistructured models often involve data types of values associated with specific elements (identified by specific *tags* in XML.) Values for lengths of strings, integers or other types of data acceptable for what the element might represent.

Constraints might also determine which elements/tags can/must be nested within which other elements/tags.

2.5 Other Data Models

In addition to the relational and semistructured models, there are many other models that have been associated with DBMS's

2.5.1 Object oriented Features

A modern trend is to add object oriented features to extend the capabilities of the relational model.

Object oriented features have two consequences in a DBMS:

Values can be structures rather than being limited to elementary types as is the norm in relational and semistructured models.

Relations can have associated methods.

A model which combines relational and object oriented features might be called an/the *object relational* model.

There are also purely object oriented database models, in which the relation is not the principal data structuring concept, but one of several. These models are not presently in wide use.

Data Models

2.5.2 Earlier Models

There are several models that were used in earlier DBMS's but have fallen out of use

2.5.2.1 The hierarchical model

The hierarchical model, like the semistructured model, was a tree oriented model, but one that operated at the physical level. This made it difficult/impossible for programmers to write high level code.

2.5.2.2 The network model

The network model was a graph oriented physical level model and had the generality of graphs built into it.

2.6 Comparing Modelling Approaches

Although, as is obvious, semistructured models are more flexible than relational models, the relational model is much more widely used.

For large databases, efficiency, both of data access and of modification, is important.

Programmer productivity is also an important factor

The relational model provides:

A simple limited approach to structuring data that is reasonably versatile and has been found to be capable of modelling just about anything.

A collection of data operations which, although limited, has been found to be adequate for the purposes of database manipulations.

It is precisely the abovementioned limitations that allow us to implement higher level languages, such as SQL.

These higher level languages allow programmers to work at a higher level.

In such languages, short programs (often only a few lines of code) can produce results that would require hundreds or even thousands of lines in other systems (C, hierarchical systems, etc.)

In addition, the limitations of the systems allow for effective compiler level optimization.

2.7 Basics of the Relational Model

The relational model has only one way of representing/describing data. All data is represented as entries in two dimensional tables (called relations.)

Figure 2-01 is an example of just such a relation.

Each *row* represents a class in the college and each *column* represents a *property* of a class at the college: ProgramID, CourseNumber, SectionNumber, TeacherIDNumber and RoomID.

We use the term "*attributes*" to describe the *meanings* of the entries in the columns. *Attribute names* appear at the tops of the columns.

Data Models

2.7.1 Schemas

The combination of the name of a relation, together with the set of attributes for the relation, are referred to as the *schema* for that relation

A schema is normally shown/defined as the relation name, together with a parenthesized list of attributes

The schema for the relation of Figure 2-01 would be:

Classes(ProgramID, CourseNumber, SectionNumber, TeacherIDNumber, RoomID)

- Note that, although it is usually convenient to display the attributes of a schema in a consistent (standard) order, the attributes form a *set*, not a *list*. The order in which they appear in the schema description is not really part of the database, but having a standard order understood for the attributes is often convenient for descriptions concerning the relation.

In a relational model, a database consists of one or more relations. The set of schemas for the relations of a database is called a *relational database schema*, or, more concisely, just a *database schema.*

2.7.2 Tuples

The rows of a relation (except for the first row: containing the attribute names) are called *tuples:*

- A tuple has one component for each attribute of the relation.

- Our example Classes relation (Figure 2-01) displays 4 tuples, each having five components:
    (COMP, 1001, 011, 744150105, TUR2003)
    (MATH, 3101, 122, 514067723, FUN101)
    (BIOL, 2212, 020, 444917012, DUP311)
    (SCLP, 4123, 161, 888991121, HUM202)

    - Notice that, when describing an individual tuple, we have no attribute headers, so we must make use of the standard order in listing the attributes.

The relational model requires that each entry in each tuple be *atomic.*

- That it must be of some elementary data type (integer, string, ...)

- It cannot be a value with a record structure (a set, a list, an array, ...)

- Each attribute has associated with it, a *domain* (a particular elementary data type.)

    All tuple entries for an attribute must be of the data type associated with that attribute (be a value from the attribute's domain.)

- It is possible (and common) to include the data types of the attributes in the schema for a relation

    Classes(
        ProgramID:string,
        CourseNumber:integer,
        SectionNumber:integer,
        TeacherIDNumber:string,
        RoomID:string
)

Data Models

2.7.3 Equivalent Representations

Relations are *sets* of tuples, not lists of tuples. The order in which the tuples are presented is immaterial (except insofar as it affects the convenience of description and/or display.)

The order in which the *attributes* of a relation are presented is also immaterial (once again, except insofar as it affects the convenience of description and/or display.)

These two tables below (Figures 2-03 and 2-04) have the same attributes (although not in the same order) and for each row in either table, there is a corresponding row in the other with the same values of each of its attributes. The tables describe exactly the same relation.

ProgramID	CourseNumber	SectionNumber	TeacherIDNumber	RoomID
BIOL	2212	020	444917012	DUP311
COMP	1001	011	744500105	TUR203
MATH	3101	122	514067723	FUN101
SCLP	4123	161	888991121	HUM202

Figure 2-03

CourseNumber	ProgramID	SectionNumber	RoomID	TeacherIDNumber
2212	BIOL	020	DUP311	444917012
4123	SCLP	161	HUM202	888991121
3101	MATH	122	FUN101	514067723
1001	COMP	011	TUR203	744500105

Figure 2-04

2.7.4 Instances of a Relation

Many relations are not static. During registration at a college, we would anticipate the values in their "Classes" table might change. New classes might be added if an unexpected number of students request a course and a class might be removed if the enrollment is unexpectedly low (or if a professor were to become sick or resign.)

It is quite common for tuples to be added to or removed from relations, or for values of entries to be modified, but it is less common for attributes to be added or removed from the schema of a relation. These kinds of changes can be very difficult to implement, especially in large databases

A set of tuples for a given relation is called an *instance* of that relation

A conventional database system will normally maintain only one active version of any relation. This version is called the *current instance* of the relation.

2.7.5 Key Constraints in Relations

The relational model supports many different kinds of constraints, but one kind of constraint is fundamental: the *key* constraint

– A set of attributes forms a *key* for a relation if no two tuples in the relation are allowed to have the same values in all the attributes of the key

– Example: In the relation of Figure 2-01

No single attribute could serve as a key.

A program would offer different courses with different course numbers, different programs might use the same course number (i.e. MATH 1001, COMP 1001, ENGL 1001) and different classes might easily have the same section number, a teacher would be assigned more than one class and different classes would meet in a given classroom (presumably not at the same time.)

In fact, no *two* attributes would serve as a key for this relation, however if two classes in the same program have the same CourseNumber, then they should have different section numbers (that is what section numbers are for) and the set

{ProgramID, CourseNumber, SectionNumber}

forms a key for the Classes relation.

15

Data Models

In creating a schema, we can use underlining to indicate that an attribute or combination of attributes forms a key.

Classes(
    ProgramID:string,
    CourseNumber:integer,
    SectionNumber:integer,
    TeacherID:string,
    RoomNumber:string
)

Note that when we state that a set of attributes forms a key for a relation, we are making an assertion about all possible instances of the relation, not just one isolated instance.

In our "Classes" example, the instance displayed (Figures 2-01, 2-03, 2-04) there is only one tuple for each value of the ProgramID attribute, so, from this sample, we might suspect that ProgramID could serve as a key. Our experience should tell us, however, that college "Programs" offer more than one course, not just one, so ProgramID cannot be used as a key.

Observations based on a single instance cannot be trusted in identifying keys for relations.

Many real world databases make use of artificial keys to guarantee attributes with unique values

Student ID numbers, Employee ID numbers, VIN numbers, ISBN numbers.

There is nothing wrong with having several alternative choices for keys:

- Faculty members have both ID numbers and social security numbers.

- Drivers have drivers' license numbers and social security numbers.

- Automobiles have both VIN numbers and license plate numbers.

2.7.6 Example Database Schema

A database will typically involve more than one relation, and each relation will have its own schema.

In this section we will construct an example *database* schema including and extending the earlier example (of Figures 2-01, 2-02, 2-03 and 2-04.)

A college/school doesn't just involve classes. It also deals with teachers and students. Further, there is also the (even more complex) factor of the interrelationships of these things:

– some teachers teach some classes and other teachers teach others

– some students are enrolled in some classes but are not enrolled in other classes.

16

Data Models

The school's database should include (representations of) records for all of these kinds of information. It might use a database with schema something like the following:

Classes(
    <u>ProgramID</u>:string,
    <u>CourseNumber</u>:integer,
    <u>SectionNumber</u>:integer,
    TeacherIDNumber:string,
    RoomID:string
)

Personnel(
    <u>IDNumber</u>:string,
    SocSec:string, string,
    LastName:string,
    FirstName:string,
    Gender:character,
)

Faculty(
    <u>IDNumber</u>:string,
    OfficeID:string,
    DeptID:string
)

Department(
    <u>DeptID</u>:string, ,
    ChairIDNumber:string,
    DeptOffice:string
)

Student(
    <u>IDNumber</u>:string,
    ProgramOfStudy:string,
    TuitionStatus:string;
    HonorStudent:boolean
)

EnrolledIn(
    <u>IDNumber</u>:string,
    <u>ProgramID</u>:string,
    <u>CourseNumber</u>:integer,
    <u>SectionNumber</u>:integer,
    EnrollmentTypeID:string
)

Data Models

Faculty members, students and all other personnel associated with the college all have names, but, since it is quite possible that there could be more than one college person with the same name, it is quite common for an institution to assign "identification numbers" to employees and students (as well as any other associated personnel) to provide unique identifications[5]. "IDNumber" will be a key for the relations "Personnel", "Faculty" and "Students". Faculty members will typically be employed by departments corresponding to their fields of study and the kinds of courses they might teach. Faculty members are also typically assigned offices where they can store their books, meet with students, prepare lectures, and, in general, do much of their work.

We assume that each *class* will be identified by the combination

(ProgramID, CourseNumber, SectionNumber)

and will be taught by a "Teacher" who can be identified by his/her TeacherIDNumber (in the "Classes" relation which must match his/her IDNumber in the "Faculty" relation.)

Students also have names and will typically be enrolled in "programs of study". Again, it is quite possible for two different students to have the same name, so it is common to assign them id numbers to ensure different students can be identified uniquely in the system.

The relationship between classes and students is fundamentally different from that between classes and teachers. Since a class would have only one teacher (which is why we can identify the teacher using an attribute in the "Classes" schema) but a class will have more than one student. We cannot use the same technique to identify students enrolled in the class. A "Student" attribute in the Class relation would require that the same class appear in more than one row of the table, one row for each student enrolled in the class. The idea of the "Classes" relation is that each class is identified by one unique row in the table.

A student would typically be enrolled in more than one class, so we cannot identify class enrollment in the "Student" table either.

In order to have a record of which student is enrolled in which class, we use a separate relation, the "EnrolledIn" relation. A row in the "EnrolledIn" table must identify the enrollment of a specific student (identified by the student's "IDNumber") and the class the student is enrolled in (identified by the combination "ProgramID", "CourseNumber" and "SectionNumber".) All four values are necessary to specify that a specific student is enrolled in a specific class. All four attributes are necessary to form a key for the "EnrolledIn" relation. Colleges typically recognize different types of enrollment (regular, auditing, pass-fail possibly others.)

2.8 Defining a Relation Schema in SQL

SQL (the official pronunciation is "sequel" but many people say "ess kyu ell") is the principal language used to describe and manipulate relational databases.

Most commercial database managers use something very similar to (although generally not identical to) SQL

---

[5]   The use of social security numbers for this function was quite common at one time, but this practice has largely been discontinued due to concerns about privacy and identity theft.

Data Models

2.8.1 SQL Sublanguages

SQL was originally based on Codd's relational algebra (see section 2.3.2). It is commonly (somewhat informally) subdivided into "sublanguages": DQL, DDL, DCL and DML.

DQL is a *Data Query* Language

DQL includes commands to obtain information from and modify data in a database.

The most common DQL statement is SELECT. This statement is used to search for information.

DDL is a *Data Definition* Language

DDL statements create, modify, and remove database objects such as tables, indexes, and users.

Common DDL statements are CREATE, ALTER, and DROP

DCL is *a Data Control Language*

used to control access to data stored in a database.

Common DCL commands are GRANT and REVOKE

And DML, a *Data Manipulation L*anguage

used for adding (inserting), deleting, and modifying (updating) data in a database.

Some common DML commands are INSERT, UPDATE and DELETE

2.8.2 SQL Relations

SQL makes a distinction between three kinds of relations:
  stored relationships, views and temporary tables.

2.8.2.1 Stored relations (tables)

Tables are the most common kind of relation dealt with in SQL.

They exist (persistently) in the database.

Their values (tuples) can be modified and queried.

They are created by the SQL statement CREATE TABLE.

2.8.2.1.1 The CREATE TABLE Statement

The CREATE TABLE statement declares a schema for a stored relation.

It assigns names for table and attributes.

It specifies data types for attributes.

It can specify keys for the relation as well as (other types of) constraints on values of tuples allowed to be stored in the relations.

2.8.2.1.1.1 Example

```
CREATE TABLE Classes(
    ProgramID: CHAR(4),
    CourseNumber:INT,
    SectionNumber:INT,
    TeacherIDNumber: CHAR(9)
        FOREIGN KEY REFERENCES Faculty (IDNumber),
    RoomID:CHAR(6)
        FOREIGN KEY REFERENCES Classroom (RoomID),
    PRIMARY KEY (ProgramID, CourseNumber, SectionNumber)
);
```

2.8.2.2 Views

Views are relations defined by computation. They are typically retained in RAM during the processing of a session, but are not stored between sessions. Rather, they are normally constructed (in whole or in part) as needed.

2.8.2.3 Temporary tables

Temporary tables are constructed by the SQL processor while executing queries and data modifications. These relations are deleted when the query or instruction has finished. They are not stored.

2.8.3 SQL Data Types

The SQL standard requires that every attribute have a specified data type.

SQL supports a number of data types.

Not all SQL implementations use exactly the same data types, but among the types most commonly supported are: character strings, bit strings, Boolean, dates and times, as well as several kinds of numerical types.

2.8.3.1 Character Strings

SQL Supports two types of character strings:

fixed length string (identified using the specification CHAR)

and variable length strings (identified using the specification VARCHAR).

2.8.3.1.1 Fixed Length Strings

Fixed length strings are identified using the specification CHAR(n) to declare a string of exactly n characters.

See the specifications of attributes ProgramID and TeacherIDNumber in the example in 2.8.2.1.1.1

SQL permits reasonable coercions between values of character string types.

Normally if a short string is assigned to a longer fixed string type, the value will be right padded with blanks

Data Models

2.8.3.1.2 Variable Length Strings

Variable length strings are identified using the specification VARCHAR(n) to declare a string of no more than n characters.

For an example, see specifications for attributes FirstName and LastName in the example in 2.8.4.1

2.8.3.2 Bit Strings

Bit strings are sequences of bits (binary digits.) They are analogous to character strings and, like character strings, can be of fixed length or of variable length.

The instruction BIT(n) specifies a bit string of length n

The instruction BIT VARYING(n) specifies a bit string of up to n bits.

2.8.3.3 BOOLEAN

The type BOOLEAN denotes an attribute whose type is logical

TRUE or FALSE

(or UNKNOWN)

2.8.3.4 Numerical Data Types

SQL supports various numerical data types:

(At least) two types of integer data and several types of floating point data.

Many of the numerical data types are somewhat system dependent.

2.8.3.4.1 Integer Types

The type INT or INTEGER denotes the standard integer types.

SHORTINT denotes similar kinds of values, but restricted to smaller values.

Exactly what values these types can represent will be governed by the number of bits used to represent the numbers and this will be implementation dependent.

2.8.3.4.2 Floating Point Data Types

Floating point numbers can be represented in a variety of ways

2.8.3.4.2.1 – FLOAT or REAL (these are officially synonyms.)

These are be used for typical floating point numbers.

2.8.3.4.2.2 DOUBLE PRECISION

This specifies floating point numbers of higher precision.

2.8.3.4.2.3 DECIMAL and/or NUMERIC

SQL provides types that are real numbers with fixed decimal points

DECIMAL(n, d) specifies numbers with n decimal digits, and with the decimal point d digits from the right.

NUMERIC is very similar to DECIMAL, but there will be differences. These differences are system dependent.

2.8.3.5 Dates and Times

Dates and times can be specified with the data types DATE and TIME respectively.

These values are stored as strings, but, of course, these strings must satisfy specific format rules in order that they can be correctly identified as specifying a date and/or time.

The DATE and TIME values can be coerced to string values and string values can be coerced to DATE and/or TIME values.

Of course the strings involved must satisfy the DATE and TIME format rules.

2.8.4 Simple Table Declarations

The simplest form of table declaration consists of the keywords CREATE TABLE followed by the name of the relation and a parenthesized, comma separated list of attributes with their data types.

2.8.4.1 Table Declarations: Example1:

Declaration creating table with the following schema:

```
Student(
    IDNumber:string,
    ProgramOfStudy:string,
    TuitionStatus:string
)
CREATE TABLE Student(
    IDNumber CHAR(9) PRIMARY KEY
        FOREIGN KEY REFERENCES Personnel(IDNumber),
    ProgramOfStudy CHAR(4),
    TuitionStatus CHAR(6)
);
```

Note that this an SQL declaration includes information not specified in the schema. (Specific string lengths and foreign key reference.)

2.8.4.2 Table Declarations: Example2:

Declaration creating table with the following schema:

```
Faculty(
    IDNumber:string,
    SocSecNum:string,
    OfficeID:string,
    DeptID:string
)
CREATE TABLE Faculty(
    IDNumber CHAR(9) PRIMARY KEY
        FOREIGN KEY REFERENCES Personnel(IDNumber),
    OfficeID CHAR(6)
        FOREIGN KEY REFERENCES Offices(OfficeID),
    DeptID VARCHAR(20)
        FOREIGN KEY REFERENCES Department(DeptID)
);
```

Again, the SQL declaration includes a great deal of information not specified in the schema.

Data Models

2.8.5   Table Declarations with Keys

In both of the above example relations, there is an attribute (designated *IDNumber* in both cases) that is clearly intended to function as a key. If we want our DBMS to enforce the restrictions involved (that is, if we want the system to reject any attempt to enter students or faculty with duplicate id numbers) then the table declaration should identify these attributes as being *keys*.

There are two ways to do this.

2.8.5.1   KEY Statement *with* Attribute Declaration

If, as in these examples, the key is a single attribute, we can simply add the "PRIMARY KEY" constraint to the attribute declaration, as we did:

```
CREATE TABLE Student(
    IDNumber CHAR(9) PRIMARY KEY
        FOREIGN KEY REFERENCES Personnel(IDNumber),
    ProgramOfStudy CHAR(4),
    TuitionStatus CHAR(6)
);
```

2.8.5.2   KEY Declaration *separate from* Attribute Declaration

An alternative is to add a separate declaration identifying the "PRIMARY KEY" as in the following:

```
CREATE TABLE Personnel(
    IDNumber CHAR(9),
    SocSecNum CHAR(9) UNIQUE,
    LastName VARCHAR(30),
    FirstName VARCHAR(25),
    Gender CHAR(1),
    PRIMARY KEY (IDNumber)
);
```

2.8.5.3   Key Declaration with Multiple Attributes

If, as will be in the case of relation "Classes", the (primary) key involves multiple attributes then the only alternative is to define the key using the separate declaration format, since it is necessary to identify all of the attributes involved in the key.

```
CREATE TABLE Classes(
    ProgramID: CHAR(4),
    CourseNumber:INT,
    SectionNumber:INT,
    TeacherIDNumber: CHAR(9)
        FOREIGN KEY REFERENCES Faculty (IDNumber),
    RoomID:CHAR(6)
        FOREIGN KEY REFERENCES Classroom (RoomID),
    PRIMARY KEY (ProgramID, CourseNumber, SectionNumber)
);
```

Data Models

2.8.5.4 UNIQUE Declarations

A table can have more than one key, but SQL will not support more than one "primary" key.

In addition to StudentID's and FacID's our students and faculty, as well as other college employees, also have social security numbers. If we include this information in the database we would want the system to prohibit duplication of these attributes, as it would prohibit duplication of values of a key. The constraint we would use to do this is "UNIQUE", since we have already chosen to use IDNumber's as primary keys.

```
CREATE TABLE Personnel(
    IDNumber CHAR(9) PRIMARY KEY,
    SocSecNum CHAR(9) UNIQUE,
    LastName VARCHAR(30),
    FirstName VARCHAR(25),
    Gender CHAR(1)
);
```

The UNIQUE constraint is declared in exactly the same way as is the PRIMARY KEY and the two function in much the same way. One important difference, however, is in the way they treat NULL values.

In the *CREATE TABLE Classes* example above (Section 2.8.5.3) with the declaration
PRIMARY KEY (ProgramID, CourseNumber, SectionNumber)
every entry in the table must have a non null value for each of the three attributes
ProgramID, CourseNumber and SectionNumber.
Any attempt to enter a row/tuple which doesn't meet this criterion will generate an error message.

If, on the other hand, we had declared
UNIQUE (ProgramID, CourseNumber, SectionNumber)
then entries with null values for one or more of these attributes would be acceptable.

2.8.6 Table Declarations with Foreign Keys

Table entries can reference entries in other tables.

In our "Classes" example in 2.8.5.3 above, it is reasonable that a value in the "TeacherIDNumber" attribute of an entry should identify an entry in the "Faculty" table.

To ensure that the values in a table do, in fact reference entries that exist in another table, we use the "FOREIGN KEY" constraint.

The "FOREIGN KEY" constraint is a requirement that values of an attribute or collection of attributes will identify an entry in another table.

Data Models

2.8.6.1 Foreign Keys with only one Attribute

A foreign key declaration must:

> > identify another (existing) table (using a "REFERENCES" statement)

> > specify (within parentheses) the attribute used to identify entries in that table.

With only one attribute the FOREIGN KEY declaration can be part of the attribute declaration.

```
CREATE TABLE Classes(
    ProgramID: CHAR(4),
    CourseNumber:INT,
    SectionNumber:INT,
    TeacherIDNumber: CHAR(9)
        FOREIGN KEY REFERENCES Faculty (IDNumber),
    RoomID:CHAR(6)
        FOREIGN KEY REFERENCES Classroom (RoomID),
    PRIMARY KEY (ProgramID, CourseNumber, SectionNumber)
);
```

The attribute referenced (*IDNumber* in this example) must identify the entries in the second table ("Faculty"), and so, the attribute must be a key for that table. It must have been declared with constraint "UNIQUE" or (preferably) "PRIMARY KEY"

The data types of the associated attributes must be at least *compatible* and it is preferable that they be identical.

2.8.6.2 Foreign Keys with Multiple Attributes

Many tables have keys involving more than one attribute (our "Classes" table is an example) and recall that in section 2.7.6 we discussed the need for a table with schema:

```
EnrolledIn(
    IDNumber:string,
    ProgramID:string,
    CourseNumber:integer,
    SectionNumber:integer,
    EnrollmentTypeID:string
)
```

In this schema, it is clear that it is the combination
    "ProgramID", "CourseNumber", "SectionNumber"
that will identify class in which the student would be enrolled.

When more than one attribute is involved, the "FOREIGN KEY" declaration must be separate from the attribute declarations.

With a separate declaration, a foreign key declaration must:

> identify the attribute(s) referencing the other table as a comma separated list within parentheses

> identify the other table (with a "REFERENCES" statement)

> specify the attributes being referenced in the other table. These should be identified as a comma separated list within parentheses.

```
CREATE TABLE EnrolledIn(
    IDNumber CHAR(9)
        FOREIGN KEY REFERENCES Student (IDNumber),
    ProgramID CHAR(4),
    CourseNumber CHAR(4),
    SectionNumber INT,
    EnrollmentTypeID VARCHAR(8),
    PRIMARY KEY (IDNumber, ProgramID, CourseNumber, SectionNumber),
    FOREIGN KEY (ProgramID, CourseNumber, SectionNumber)
        REFERENCES Classes (ProgramID, CourseNumber, SectionNumber)
);
```

Again, the combination of attributes being *referenced* must have been declared as either "UNIQUE" or "PRIMARY KEY"

2.8.7 Modifying a Relation Schema

If we need to, we can modify the schema of a database (even after it has been in use and has tuples in its current instance.)

The most serious modification would be the complete elimination of a relation.

Other structural modifications would involve eliminating a table *attribute*, adding a *new* attribute or changing the *data type* of an attribute.

2.8.7.1 The DROP TABLE command

The elimination of a relation can be accomplished with the "DROP TABLE" command:

The command DROP TABLE *R* simply eliminates the relation *R*

Example:

DROP TABLE Student

would eliminate the table "Student" from the database.

There are *limitations* on the DROP TABLE command:

If the table is referenced in a FOREIGN KEY constraint in another table, the DROP TABLE command cannot be executed and the DBMS will report an error.

Some systems report an error if the table being dropped does not exist. These systems, however, also support an "IF EXISTS" option.

A few systems will only execute a DROP TABLE command if the table is empty

– "empty" meaning has no tuples.

2.8.7.2   The ALTER TABLE command

Removing an entire table is not done very often.

More commonly, one will want to modify the structure of an existing table. We might want to add new attributes and/or remove existing attributes to/from the relation, and/or we might want to change the data types of existing attributes. To do any of these things we use the command ALTER TABLE

The ALTER TABLE instruction must identify the relation to be modified and must identify the changes to be made.

The changes that might be made in the structure of a relation include:

removal of an attribute (DROP)

addition of a new attribute (ADD)

change of characteristic(s) of existing attribute(s) (MODIFY)

2.8.7.2.1   The ALTER TABLE command DROP

The ALTER TABLE command has a DROP option that will remove an attribute from the table schema and delete any values of that attribute that might already be stored in the tuples in the relation.

EXAMPLE: Since social security numbers are more and more being involved in identity theft, somebody might decide that they should be stored in a separate file where access to the information could be better protected.

CREATE TABLE SocialSecurityTable(
    IDNumber CHAR(9) PRIMARY KEY,
    SocSecNum CHAR(9) UNIQUE,
    FOREIGN KEY IDNumber References Personnel(IDNumber)
);

ALTER TABLE Personnel DROP SocSecNum;

2.8.7.2.2   The ALTER TABLE command MODIFY option

The MODIFY option of the ALTER TABLE command is used to *change* the properties of an attribute.

EXAMPLE: In our CREATE TABLE statements above, the "CourseNumber" attributes in the "EnrolledIn" and the "Classes" tables do not match. At least one of those must be changed.

ALTER TABLE Classes MODIFY CourseNumber CHAR(4)

Data Models

2.8.7.2.3   The ALTER TABLE command ADD

The ADD option results in a new attribute in the table.

When we execute an
    ALTER TABLE Demo… ADD …
and the table "Demo" already has data entered in it, each of the existing rows in the table will now have the new attribute(s). The value(s) of that/those attribute(s) for the existing elements will be the default value NULL.

If we want those values to be some other value can add a DEFAULT option to the ALTER TABLE … ADD … command.

EXAMPLE:

ALTER TABLE Student ADD HonorStudent boolean DEFAULT false;

2.9 Example System:

For our future examples, we will be referring frequently to a database created with the following structure:

CREATE TABLE SocialSecurityTable(
    IDNumber CHAR(9) PRIMARY KEY,
    SocSecNum CHAR(9) UNIQUE,
    FOREIGN KEY IDNumber References Personnel(IDNumber)
);

CREATE TABLE Personnel(
    IDNumber CHAR(9) PRIMARY KEY,
    LastName VARCHAR(30),
    FirstName VARCHAR(25),
    Gender CHAR(1)
);

CREATE TABLE Program(
    ProgramID CHAR(4) PRIMARY KEY,
    DeptID CHAR(4) FOREIGN KEY REFERENCES Department (DeptID)
);

CREATE TABLE Course(
    ProgramID CHAR(4) FOREIGN KEY REFERENCES Program (ProgramID),
    CourseNumber CHAR(4),
    Credits INT,
    PRIMARY KEY (ProgramID, CourseNumber)
);

CREATE TABLE Offices(
    OfficeID CHAR(6) PRIMARY KEY,
    OfficePhone CHAR(4) UNIQUE
);

Data Models

```
CREATE TABLE ClassRoom(
    RoomID CHAR(6) Primary KEY,
    Capacity INT
);

CREATE TABLE Faculty(
    IDNumber CHAR(9)
        PRIMARY KEY
        FOREIGN KEY REFERENCES Personnel (IDNumber),
    Office CHAR(6) FOREIGN KEY REFERENCES Offices (OfficeID),
    Dept CHAR(4) FOREIGN KEY REFERENCES Department (DeptID)
);

CREATE TABLE Student(
    IDNumber CHAR(9)
        PRIMARY KEY
        FOREIGN KEY REFERENCES Personnel (IDNumber),
    ProgramOfStudy(CHAR(4) ) FOREIGN KEY REFERENCES Program (ProgramID),
    TuitionStatus VARCHAR(10),
    HonorStudent BOOLEAN
);

CREATE TABLE Classes(
    ProgramID: CHAR(4),
    CourseNumber:CHAR(4),
    SectionNumber:CHAR(3),
    TeacherIDNumber: CHAR(9)
        FOREIGN KEY REFERENCES Faculty (IDNumber),
    RoomID:CHAR(6)
        FOREIGN KEY REFERENCES Classroom (RoomID),
    PRIMARY KEY (ProgramID, CourseNumber, SectionNumber)
);

CREATE TABLE EnrolledIn(
    IDNumber: CHAR(9) FOREIGN KEY REFERENCES Student (IDNumber),
    ProgramID: CHAR(4),
    CourseNumber: CHAR(4),
    SectionNumber: CHAR(3),
    PRIMARY KEY (StudentID, ProgramID, CourseNumber, SectionNumber),
    FOREIGN KEY (ProgramID, CourseNumber, SectionNumber)
        REFERENCES Classes (ProgramID, CourseNumber, SectionNumber)
);

CREATE TABLE Department(
    DeptID CHAR(4) PRIMARY KEY,
    OfficeID CHAR(6),
    DeptChair CHAR(9)
        FOREIGN KEY REFERENCES Faculty (IDNumber)
);
```

Data Models

2.10 Example Instance of Database with Above Example Schema

Program

ProgramID	DeptID
COMP	Math
MATH	Math
STAT	Math
SPAN	Lang
GRMN	Lang
RUSS	Lang
BIOL	Scie
PHYS	Scie
GEOL	Scie
SCLP	Huma
GRAF	Huma

Course

ProgramID	CourseNumber	Credits
COMP	1001	3
MATH	3101	4
BIOL	2212	3
SCLP	4123	3

ClassRoom

RoomID	Capacity
DUP311	122
FUN101	32
HUM202	16
TUR203	24

Offices

OfficeID	OfficePhone
DUP101	3401
DUP409	3434
DUP411	3481
DUP510	3460
FOR102	2001
FOR403	6323
HUM207	5002
HUM504	5223
MTH323	6552
TUR104	3901
TUR411	3921

Faculty

IDNumber	OfficeID	DeptID
444917012	DUP409	Scie
614726215	DUP411	Scie
514067723	MTH323	Math
744150105	TUR411	Math
521788724	DUP510	Scie
601552112	FOR403	Lang
888991121	HUM504	Huma

Student

IDNumber	ProgramOfStudy	HonorStudent	TuitionStatus
801428821	SCLP	TRUE	Paid
803526671	SPAN	FALSE	Paid
802465401	BIOL	FALSE	Paid
801488722	BIOL	TRUE	Paid

Personnel

IDNumber	LastName	FirstName	Gender
444917012	Smith	Samuel	M
614726215	Oatie	Donkey	M
514067723	Johnson	Robert	M
744150105	Watanabe	Kimberly	F
521788724	Avvoltoio	Victoria	F
601552112	Beamish	John	M
888991121	Hare	Harvey	M
801428821	Reller	Cindy	F
803526671	Lugo	Belinda	F
802465401	Panda	Sancho	M
801488722	Rabbit	Jack	M

SocialSecurityTable

IDNumber	SocSec
444917012	212325561
614726215	655872435
514067723	774123571
744150105	257553714
521788724	785247415
601552112	335247864
888991121	545336921
801428821	623554503
803526671	547219965
802465401	777953021
801488722	696756968

Classes

ProgramID	CourseNumber	SectionNumber	TeacherIDNumber	RoomID
BIOL	2212	020	444917012	DUP311
COMP	1001	011	744500105	TUR203
MATH	3101	122	514067723	FUN101
SCLP	4123	161	888991121	HUM202

EnrolledIn

ProgramID	CourseNumber	SectionNumber	IDNumber
SCLP	4123	161	801428821
BIOL	2212	020	801488722
COMP	1001	011	802465401

Department

DeptID	OfficeID	DeptChair
Math	TUR104	744150105
Lang	FOR102	601552112
Scie	DUP101	521788724
Huma	HUM108	888991121

Data Models

2.11 Chapter 2 Questions:

    2.11.1 TRUE/FALSE

        2.11.1.1 Semistructured models are more flexible than relational models

        2.11.1.2 The *relational* model is more widely used in DBMS's than semistructured models

        2.11.1.3 The *relational* model is more widely used in DBMS's than semistructured models

        2.11.1.4 The attributes of a relation form a *set*, not a *list*

        2.11.1.5 The type CHAR(n) declares a fixed length string of n characters

        2.11.1.6 SQL does not permit coercions between values of character string types

    2.11.2 MULTIPLE CHOICE

        2.11.2.1 An important concept involved in data models is
- a. Structure of data
- b. Operations on data
- c. Constraints on data
- d. all of the above
- e. none of the above

        2.11.2.2 The simplest form of declaration schema consists of the keywords _____ TABLE followed by the name of the relation and a parenthesized, comma separated list of attributes with their data types
- a. MAKE
- b. DECLARE
- c. CREATE
- d. DEFINE
- e. none of the above

    2.11.3 COMPLETION

        2.11.3.1 The notion of a data _____ is fundamental to the study of database systems

        2.11.3.2 Data models/database implementations typically involve structures, operations, constraints specific to database/data models and at this level, the structures are referred to as the _____ model.

        2.11.3.3 In a database data model, operations that retrieve information are referred to as

        _____

        2.11.3.4 There are two important data models in wide use today:

    –   The relational model is present in all commercial database systems and when people talk about "databases" and "database systems" this is the one they are probably talking about

        –   Can also include object-oriented extensions

    –   The _____ model

        •   XML is the primary manifestation of this model.

Data Models

2.11.3.5 The relational database model is based on _____

2.11.3.6 The _____ database model resembles trees or graphs rather than tables or arrays

2.11.3.7 A modern trend is to add _____ oriented features to the relational model

2.11.3.8 There are several models that were used in earlier DBMS's but have fallen out of use.
  - The hierarchical model
    - Like the semistructured model was a tree oriented model, but operated at the physical level which made it difficult/impossible for programmers to write high level code.
  - The _____ model
    - Was a graph oriented physical level model. The generality of graphs was built into this model

2.11.3.9 We use the term "_____" to describe the *meanings* of the entries in the columns

2.11.3.10 The name of a relation together with the set of attributes for the relation, are referred to as the _____ for that relation

2.11.3.11 The relational model requires that each entry in each tuple be _____

2.11.3.12 A set of tuples for a given relation is called a (n) _____ of that relation

2.11.3.13 _____ is the principal language used to describe and manipulate relational databases

2.11.3.14 There are two aspects to (sublanguages of) SQL
  - The *Data-Definition* sublanguage
    - For declaring database schemas
  - The *Data-*_____ sublanguage
    - For querying (asking questions of) and for modifying a database

2.11.3.15 SQL makes a distinction between three kinds of relations:
  - Stored relations (tables)
    - The most common kind of relation
    - A relation that exists in the database, can be modified (by changing its tuples) and can be queried
    - The CREATE TABLE statement declares a schema for a stored relation
      - Assigns names for table and attributes. Specifies data types for attributes. Specifies keys.

  - _____
    - Relations defined by computation
    - Not stored, but constructed (in whole or in part) when needed
  - Temporary tables
    - Constructed by the SQL processor while executing queries and data modifications
      - These relations are thrown away, not stored

2.11.3.16 There are two declarations that can be used to indicate keys:
  - PRIMARY KEY
  - _____

Chapter 3 Algebraic Query Language

A functional database system requires more than just the capability for storing data. It also requires the capability for updating the information and for "*querying*" the database i.e. communicating with the database and getting information out of it that the users want.

The underlying structure that supports our system of querying and modifying data is a *relational algebra* consisting of simple but effective ways to construct new relations from given relations. When the given relations are stored data, the constructed relations can be results of *queries* about this data.

The relational algebra is not used directly by a DBMS, but is built into the 'real' query languages, such as SQL. When a DBMS processes an SQL query, the first thing it does is convert it into a relational algebra expression (or something similar.)

3.1   Why Do We Need a "*Query Language*"

One could, of course, use a high level language (C, C++, FORTRAN, Java, …) to create, and retrieve information, from a database system. However, programs to do this would be extremely complex. They would involve quite a bit of "*re-inventing the wheel*".

Specialized languages designed specifically for database management (primarily SQL and related languages) are easier for programmers to use. They are also easier for compilers to optimize.

3.2   Relational Algebra and Database Queries

It was Codd who, in 1970, formulated the relational model for database management that became the basis for relational database management systems. This relational algebra provides a formal structure for describing precisely what actions the DBMS performs and precisely what they do. It aids in the design of compilers for the system language and provides a system for determining whether they are correct. It also supports the optimization of implementing actions/programs in the language.

3.2.1   What is an Algebra

In general, algebras involve both *values* and *operands.*

The most familiar example of an algebra would be the *arithmetic* algebra.

The <u>operands</u> in the arithmetic algebra are variables (x, y, i, n, …)

These variables represent numbers.

The <u>operators</u> in the arithmetic algebra are the familiar arithmetic operators: addition, subtraction, multiplication and division.

Any algebra allows us to build expressions by applying operations to operands and/or other expressions

Usually parentheses are necessary to group operators and operands

$(x + 3) / (x - 7)$

Algebraic Query Language

3.2.2 Relational Algebra

The *relational algebra* (originally described by Codd) is another example of an algebra

The relational algebra *operands* are:

1. Variables (that stand for relations)
2. Constants (that are finite relations)

The *operations* of (the traditional) relational algebra fall into four broad categories:

– Set operations:
  - Union, intersection and difference
– Operations that remove parts of relations
  - *Selection;* that eliminates some rows.
  - *Projection;* that eliminates some columns.
– Operations that combine relations
  - Cartesian products and various "join" operations
– Renaming.
  - An operation that does not change the tuples of a relation but changes the names of attributes and/or the relation itself

We will generally refer to relational algebra expressions as *queries*

3.2.2.1 Set Operations

The three most common set operations are union, intersection and difference.

Set operations can, of course, be performed on arbitrary sets, not just relations

– R∪S, the union of R and S, is the collection of elements that are in R, in S, or in both.
– R∩S, the intersection of R and S, is the collection of all elements that are both in R and in S.
– R-S, the difference of R and S, is the collection of elements that are in R but not in S

Notice that the difference operation is different from union and intersection in one important way:

– R∪S = S∪R and R∩S = S∩R, but R-S is generally different from S-R

In order to apply set operations to (database) relations in a meaningful way, we must make some assumptions about the sets R and S

– R and S are sets of tuples
– R and S have schemas with identical sets of attributes and the types for each attribute must be the same for both R and S
– The columns for both R and S must be ordered with the same order for both R and S

Sometimes we will want to compute union, intersection and/or difference for relations with the same number of attributes which have the same types (domains) but different names.

– In this case we can use the "renaming" operator

3.2.2.2 Set Operation Examples 1

Assuming R is the relation:

R	
C1	C2
E1	1
E2	2
E3	3

And S is the relation

S	
C1	C2
E2	2
E3	3
E4	4

3.2.2.2.1 The union R∪S is the relation

R∪S	
C1	C2
E1	1
E2	2
E3	3
E4	4

3.2.2.2.2 The intersection R∩S is

R∩S	
C1	C2
E2	2
E3	3

3.2.2.2.3 The difference R-S is

R-S	
C1	C2
E1	1

3.2.2.3 Set Operation Examples 2

Assuming R is the relation

R				
IDNumber	SocSec	LastName	FirstName	Gender
444917012	212325561	Smith	Samuel	M
614726215	655872435	Oatie	Donkey	M
514067723	774123571	Johnson	Robert	M
744150105	257553714	Watanabe	Kimberly	F
521788724	785247415	Avvoltoio	Victoria	F
601552112	335247864	Beamish	John	M
888991121	545336921	Hare	Harvey	M

And S is the relation

S				
IDNumber	SocSec	LastName	FirstName	Gender
521788724	785247415	Avvoltoio	Victoria	F
601552112	335247864	Beamish	John	M
888991121	545336921	Hare	Harvey	M
801428821	623554503	Reller	Cindy	F
803526671	547219965	Lugo	Belinda	F
802465401	777953021	Panda	Sancho	M
801488722	696756968	Rabbit	Jack	M

3.2.2.3.1 The union R∪S would be the relation

RUS				
IDNumber	SocSec	LastName	FirstName	Gender
444917012	212325561	Smith	Samuel	M
614726215	655872435	Oatie	Donkey	M
514067723	774123571	Johnson	Robert	M
744150105	257553714	Watanabe	Kimberly	F
521788724	785247415	Avvoltoio	Victoria	F
601552112	335247864	Beamish	John	M
888991121	545336921	Hare	Harvey	M
801428821	623554503	Reller	Cindy	F
803526671	547219965	Lugo	Belinda	F
802465401	777953021	Panda	Sancho	M
801488722	696756968	Rabbit	Jack	M

3.2.2.3.2 The intersection R∩S would be the relation

R∩S				
IDNumber	SocSec	LastName	FirstName	Gender
521788724	785247415	Avvoltoio	Victoria	F
601552112	335247864	Beamish	John	M
888991121	545336921	Hare	Harvey	M

3.2.2.3.3 The difference R-S would be the relation

R-S				
IDNumber	SocSec	LastName	FirstName	Gender
444917012	212325561	Smith	Samuel	M
614726215	655872435	Oatie	Donkey	M
514067723	774123571	Johnson	Robert	M
744150105	257553714	Watanabe	Kimberly	F

3.2.2.4 The Projection Operation

The projection operator is used to produce a new relation that has only some of the attributes of the original relation.

We use the symbol π to identify the projection operator. The attributes that the projection retains are listed as a subscript of the symbol.

$\pi_{A,B,C}(R)$ is the relation/table that has all the entries from R that are in columns A, B and C

Assuming again. as in 3.2.2.3, that R is the relation

R				
IDNumber	SocSec	LastName	FirstName	Gender
444917012	212325561	Smith	Samuel	M
614726215	655872435	Oatie	Donkey	M
514067723	774123571	Johnson	Robert	M
744150105	257553714	Watanabe	Kimberly	F
521788724	785247415	Avvoltoio	Victoria	F
601552112	335247864	Beamish	John	M
888991121	545336921	Hare	Harvey	M

Then the projection $\pi_{\text{IDNumber, LastName, Gender}}(R)$ would yield the relation

$\pi_{\text{IDNumber, LastName, Gender}}$		
IDNumber	LastName	Gender
444917012	Smith	M
614726215	Oatie	M
514067723	Johnson	M
744150105	Watanabe	F
521788724	Avvoltoio	F
601552112	Beamish	M
888991121	Hare	M

3.2.2.5 The Selection Operation

The selection operator, when applied to a relation R, produces a new relation with a subset of the tuples of R (and all of the attributes of R) The tuples in the resulting operation will be those satisfying some condition C involving attributes of R,

We use the symbol σ to designate the selection operator, with the condition as a subscript.

The selection operation with condition C would be identified as $\sigma_C(R)$

The schema for the relation resulting from the selection $\sigma_C(R)$ will be the same as that for R

We typically prefer to show the attributes for $\sigma_C(R)$ in the same order as used for R

When computing a selection operation, $\sigma_C(R)$, the condition C will be a conditional expression similar to that found in most conventional programming languages. The operands in the condition C will be constants and/or attributes of the relation R. We apply the condition C to each tuple t in R by substituting all attribute values in t into the corresponding operand in the expression C (assuming there is such an operand in C.) If the resulting expression is "true", then the tuple t will be in the relation $\sigma_C(R)$ and if it is "false" then the tuple t will not be in $\sigma_C(R)$.

3.2.2.5.1 Example:

If R is the relation from 3.2.2.3 above, and C is the condition Gender = 'M' then the selection $\sigma_C(R)$ will create the relation:

$\sigma_C(R)$				
IDNumber	SocSec	LastName	FirstName	Gender
444917012	212325561	Smith	Samuel	M
614726215	655872435	Oatie	Donkey	M
514067723	774123571	Johnson	Robert	M
601552112	335247864	Beamish	John	M
888991121	545336921	Hare	Harvey	M

3.2.2.5.2 Example:

With relations R and S from 3.2.2.3 above, the selection $\sigma_{Gender = 'F'}(R \cup S)$ produces the relation:

$\sigma_{Gender = 'F'}(R \cup S)$				
IDNumber	SocSec	LastName	FirstName	Gender
744150105	257553714	Watanabe	Kimberly	F
521788724	785247415	Avvoltoio	Victoria	F
801428821	623554503	Reller	Cindy	F
803526671	547219965	Lugo	Belinda	F

3.2.2.6 The Cartesian Product

The *Cartesian Product* (or *cross product* or just *product*) of two sets, R×S, is the set of all pairs (x, y) where x∈R and y∈S

In the case that R and S are relations, then x and y are tuples,
    (x1, x2, …, xm) and (y1, y2, …, yn)
and the pair (x, y) can be considered to be a tuple (x1, x2, …, xm, y1, y2, …, yn)

and the product R×S will be a relation.

The schema for the relation R×S is the union of the schemas for R and S

but if R and S have attributes with the same names, then we will need to distinguish between the similarly named attributes from the different relations.

We do this by using dot notation:

if A is a common name for attributes in relation R and S, then we identify R.A and S.A

3.2.2.6.1 Example

Using the relations R and S from 3.2.2.2 above, the schema for the product R×S would be

R×S(
    R.C1 CHAR(2),
    R.C2 INTEGER,
    S.C1 CHAR(2),
    S.C2 INTEGER
)

And the relation R×S would be as shown at the right:

R×S			
R.C1	R.C2	S.C1	S.C2
E1	1	E2	2
E1	1	E3	3
E1	1	E4	4
E2	2	E2	2
E2	2	E3	3
E2	2	E4	4
E3	3	E2	2
E3	3	E3	3
E3	3	E4	4

3.2.2.7 The Natural Join

Very often, when two relations, R and S, have attributes with the same names, these attributes will, in fact, refer to the same properties.

In this case, the attribute values would be repeated (unnecessarily) in the Cartesian product R×S.

Rather than forming the complete Cartesian product R×S [of ALL pairs (r,s)], we might instead form the *natural* join of R and S (denoted R⋈S) in which the common attributes appear only once.

Assume that the R attributes are:
   {A1, A2, ... , An, B1, B2, ... , Bm}
and that the S attributes are:
   {A1, A2, ... , An, E1, E2, ... , Ek}
Then the attributes of R⋈S will be:
   {A1, A2, ... , An, B1, B2, ... , Bm, E1, E2, ... , Ek}
and an element of R⋈S will be a tuple of the form
   (t1, t2, ... , tn, u1, u2, ..., um, v1, v2, ..., vk)
where (t1, t2, ... , tn, u1, u2, ... , um) is a tuple in R and (t1, t2, ... , tn, v1, v2, ... , vk) is a tuple in S.

The attribute set for R⋈S is the union of the attribute sets for R and S.

A tuple in R⋈S (called a joined tuple) is the result of pairing a tuple in R and a tuple in S with attribute values the same for all common attributes.

3.2.2.7.1 Example:

Recall (from 2.10) that relations "Faculty" and "Offices are as shown here

Faculty		
IDNumber	OfficeID	DeptID
444917012	DUP409	Scie
614726215	DUP411	Scie
514067723	MTH323	Math
744150105	TUR411	Math
521788724	DUP510	Scie
601552112	FOR403	Lang
888991121	HUM504	Huma

Offices	
OfficeID	OfficePhone
DUP101	3401
DUP409	3434
DUP411	3481
DUP510	3460
FOR102	2001
FOR403	6323
HUM207	5002
HUM504	5223
MTH323	6552
TUR104	3901
TUR411	3921

These relations have common attribute OfficeID.

The relation Faculty⋈Offices would be:

Faculty ⋈ Offices			
IDNumber	OfficeID	DeptID	OfficePhone
444917012	DUP409	Scie	3434
614726215	DUP411	Scie	3481
514067723	MTH323	Math	6552
744150105	TUR411	Math	3921
521788724	DUP510	Scie	3460
601552112	FOR403	Lang	6323
888991121	HUM504	Huma	5223

3.2.2.8 The "Theta" Join

The natural join pairs tuples from two relations subject to the condition that their attribute values agree on common attributes.

Sometimes it is desirable to join tuples subject to other conditions than just having the same values for common attributes. The concept of "theta" join serves this purpose[6].

The theta join of R and S based on a condition Θ is written $R\bowtie_\Theta S$.

The result of $R\bowtie_\Theta S$ is calculated as follows:

o   Calculate the cross product R×S

o   Select from R×S only those tuples that satisfy condition Θ, and the resulting collection of tuples is $R\bowtie_\Theta S$

From this construction, it is clear that the schema for $R\bowtie_\Theta S$ is the same as that for the product R×S

3.2.2.8.1 Example of Theta Join

Consider the relations "Department" and "Faculty" A natural relationship condition Θ for these relations would be that DeptChair=IDNumber.

Department		
DeptID	OfficeID	DeptChair
Math	TUR104	744150105
Lang	FOR102	601552112
Scie	DUP101	521788724
Huma	HUM108	888991121

Faculty		
IDNumber	OfficeID	DeptID
444917012	DUP409	Scie
614726215	DUP411	Scie
514067723	MTH323	Math
744150105	TUR411	Math
521788724	DUP510	Scie
601552112	FOR403	Lang
888991121	HUM504	Huma

---

[6]   (the term theta [Θ] has historically been used to identify an arbitrary condition)

To calculate the theta join for of these relations with this condition

Department$\bowtie_\Theta$Faculty

we first construct the cross product Department×Faculty

Department×Faculty					
DeptID	OfficeID	DeptChair	IDNumber	OfficeID	DeptID
Math	TUR104	744150105	44917012	DUP409	Scie
Math	TUR104	744150105	514726215	DUP411	Scie
Math	TUR104	744150105	514067723	MTH323	Math
Math	TUR104	744150105	744150105	TUR411	Math
Math	TUR104	744150105	521788724	DUP510	Scie
Math	TUR104	744150105	601552112	FOR403	Lang
Math	TUR104	744150105	888991121	HUM504	Huma
Lang	FOR102	601552112	44917012	DUP409	Scie
Lang	FOR102	601552112	514726215	DUP411	Scie
Lang	FOR102	601552112	514067723	MTH323	Math
Lang	FOR102	601552112	744150105	TUR411	Math
Lang	FOR102	601552112	521788724	DUP510	Scie
Lang	FOR102	601552112	601552112	FOR403	Lang
Lang	FOR102	601552112	888991121	HUM504	Huma
Scie	DUP101	521788724	44491701:	DUP409	Scie
Scie	DUP101	521788724	61472621!	DUP411	Scie
Scie	DUP101	521788724	51406772!	MTH323	Math
Scie	DUP101	521788724	74415010!	TUR411	Math
Scie	DUP101	521788724	52178872|	DUP510	Scie
Scie	DUP101	521788724	60155211:	FOR403	Lang
Scie	DUP101	521788724	888991121	HUM504	Huma
Huma	HUM108	888991121	44917012	DUP409	Scie
Huma	HUM108	888991121	514726215	DUP411	Scie
Huma	HUM108	888991121	514067723	MTH323	Math
Huma	HUM108	888991121	744150105	TUR411	Math
Huma	HUM108	888991121	521788724	DUP510	Scie
Huma	HUM108	888991121	601552112	FOR403	Lang
Huma	HUM108	888991121	888991121	HUM504	Huma

And then eliminate the rows that do not satisfy the condition Θ.

This would leave:

Department$\bowtie_\Theta$Faculty					
DeptID	OfficeID	DeptChair	IDNumber	OfficeID	DeptID
Math	TUR104	744150105	744150105	TUR411	Math
Lang	FOR102	601552112	601552112	FOR403	Lang
Scie	DUP101	521788724	521788724	DUP510	Scie
Huma	HUM108	888991121	888991121	HUM504	Huma

3.3 Algebraic Query Language

Codd's relational algebra allows the formation of expressions of arbitrary complexity, by applying operations to results of other operations[7].

3.3.1 Parenthesized Expressions

The construction of complex expressions will often require the use of parentheses to specify the order in which operations are applied.

3.3.1.1 Parenthesized Example 1

Suppose we wanted a list of classes taught by professors of the Math or Huma departments at our fictional college (schemas and instance of 2.9 and 2.10)

---

[7]   As do all algebras.

Algebraic Query Language

We might begin by constructing a table of classes and their teachers (including records of the *departments* of the *teachers* which might be different from the programs of the courses.)

$$Classes \bowtie_{TeacherID=IDNumber} Faculty$$

ProgramID	CourseNumber	SectionNumber	TeacherIDNumber	RoomID	IDNumber	OfficeID	DeptID
BIOL	2212	020	444917012	DUP311	444917012	DUP409	Scie
MATH	3101	122	514067723	FUN101	514067723	MTH323	Math
COMP	1001	011	744500105	TUR203	744150105	TUR411	Math
SCLP	4123	161	888991121	HUM202	888991121	HUM504	Huma

From this table, we must select the rows with DeptID = 'Math'

$$\sigma_{DeptID='Math'}(Classes \bowtie_{TeacherIDNumber=IDNumber} Faculty)$$

ProgramID	CourseNumber	SectionNumber	TeacherIDNumber	RoomID	IDNumber	OfficeID	DeptID
MATH	3101	122	514067723	FUN101	514067723	MTH323	Math
COMP	1001	011	744500105	TUR203	744150105	TUR411	Math

and those with DeptID = 'Huma'.

$$\sigma_{Department='Huma'}(Classes \bowtie_{TeacherIDNumber=IDNumber} Faculty)$$

ProgramID	CourseNumber	SectionNumber	TeacherIDNumber	RoomID	IDNumber	OfficeID	DeptID
SCLP	4123	161	888991121	HUM202	888991121	HUM504	Huma

It is the union of these two relations is the relation we want:

$$(\sigma_{Department='Math'}(Classes \bowtie_{TeacherIDNumber=IDNumber} Faculty)) \cup (\sigma_{Department='Huma'}(Classes \bowtie_{TeacherIDNumber=IDNumber} Faculty))$$

ProgramID	CourseNumber	SectionNumber	TeacherIDNumber	RoomID	IDNumber	OfficeID	DeptID
MATH	3101	122	514067723	FUN101	514067723	MTH323	Math
COMP	1001	011	744500105	TUR203	744150105	TUR411	Math
SCLP	4123	161	888991121	HUM202	888991121	HUM504	Huma

Finally, the product Classes×Faculty has several unnecessary attributes so we might calculate the projection $\pi_{ProgramID,CourseNumber,SectionNumber}$:

$$\pi_{ProgramID,CourseNumber,SectionNumber}((\sigma_{Department='Math'}(Classes \bowtie_{TeacherIDNumber=IDNumber} Faculty)) \cup (\sigma_{Department='Huma'}(Classes \bowtie_{TeacherIDNumber=IDNumber} Faculty)))$$

ProgramID	CourseNumber	SectionNumber
MATH	3101	122
COMP	1001	011
SCLP	4123	161

3.3.1.2 Parenthesized Example 2

If we were to want a list of all students enrolled in classes taught by male professors:

We would first want a table with all of the classes taught by male professors. For this we might use the theta join $\bowtie_{TeacherIDNumber=IDNumber}$:

$$Classes \bowtie_{TeacherIDNumber=IDNumber} Personnel$$

			Classes$\bowtie_{TeacherIDNumber=IDNumber}$Personnel						
ProgramID	CourseNumber	SectionNumber	TeacherIDNumber	RoomID	IDNumber	SocSec	LastName	FirstName	Gender
BIOL	2212	020	444917012	DUP311	444917012	212325561	Smith	Samuel	M
MATH	3101	122	514067723	FUN101	514067723	774123571	Johnson	Robert	M
COMP	1001	011	744150105	TUR203	744150105	257553714	Watanabe	Kimberly	F
SCLP	4123	161	888991121	HUM202	888991121	545336921	Hare	Harvey	M

followed by selection $\sigma_{Gender='M'}$:

$$\sigma_{Gender='M'}(Classes \bowtie_{TeacherIDNumber=IDNumber} Personnel)$$

			$\sigma_{Gender='M'}$(Classes$\bowtie_{TeacherIDNumber=IDNumber}$Personnel)						
ProgramID	CourseNumber	SectionNumber	TeacherIDNumber	RoomID	IDNumber	SocSec	LastName	FirstName	Gender
BIOL	2212	020	444917012	DUP311	444917012	212325561	Smith	Samuel	M
MATH	3101	122	514067723	FUN101	514067723	774123571	Johnson	Robert	M
SCLP	4123	161	888991121	HUM202	888991121	545336921	Hare	Harvey	M

The "EnrolledIn" relation and the "Classes" relation use the same attribute names to identify classes, so we combine them using a natural join:

$$EnrolledIn \bowtie (\sigma_{Gender='M'}(Classes \bowtie_{TeacherIDNumber=IDNumber} Personnel))$$

			EnrolledIn$\bowtie$ ($\sigma_{Gender='M'}$(Classes$\bowtie_{TeacherIDNumber=IDNumber}$Personnel))						
ProgramID	CourseNumber	SectionNumber	EnrolledIn.IDNumber	TeacherIDNumber	RoomID	Personnel.IDNumber	SocSec	LastName	FirstName	Gender
SCLP	4123	161	801428821	888991121	HUM202	888991121	545336921	Hare	Harvey	M
BIOL	2212	020	801488722	444917012	DUP311	444917012	212325561	Smith	Samuel	M

This relation includes a lot of unnecessary information. All we are interested in are the students and the classes, not the teachers or classrooms. We can use the projection operator $\pi_{ProgramID,CourseNumber,SectionNumber,EnrolledIn.IDNumber}$ to produce a much simpler relation.

$$\pi_{ProgramID,CourseNumber,SectionNumber,EnrolledIn.IDNumber}(EnrolledIn \bowtie (\sigma_{Gender='M'}(Classes \bowtie_{TeacherIDNumber=IDNumber} Personnel)))$$

$\pi_{ProgramID,CourseNumber,SectionNumber,EnrolledIn.IDNumber}$(EnrolledIn$\bowtie$($\sigma_{Gender='M'}$(Classes$\bowtie_{TeacherIDNumber=IDNumber}$Personnel)))			
ProgramID	CourseNumber	SectionNumber	EnrolledIn.IDNumber
SCLP	4123	161	801428821
BIOL	2212	020	801488722

This identifies the students by their student ID number (EnrolledIn.IDNumber) and we would probably prefer to identify them using their names. Their names are in the "Personnel" relation, so we will want:

$$Personnel \bowtie_{Personnel.IDNumber=EnrolledIn.IDNumber} ($$
$$\pi_{ProgramID,CourseNumber,SectionNumber,EnrolledIn.IDNumber}($$
$$EnrolledIn \bowtie (\sigma_{Gender='M'}(Classes \bowtie_{TeacherIDNumber=IDNumber} Personnel))$$
$$)$$
$$)$$
$$);$$

Personnel.IDNumber	SocSec	LastName	FirstName	Gender	ProgramID	CourseNumber	SectionNumber	EnrolledIn.IDNumber
801428821	623554503	Reller	Cindy	F	SCLP	4123	161	801428821
801488722	696756968	Rabbit	Jack	M	BIOL	2212	020	801488722

3.3.2 Representation of Expressions using Trees

It is also possible to represent expressions in graphical form as expression *trees* (sometimes easier for humans to read and understand)

3.3.2.1 Tree Example 1

The computation of earlier example 3.3.1.1:

$$\pi_{ProgramID,CourseNumber,SectionNumber}((\sigma_{Department='Math'}(Classes \bowtie_{TeacherIDNumber=IDNumber} Faculty)) \cup (\sigma_{Department='Huma'}(Classes \bowtie_{TeacherIDNumber=IDNumber} Faculty)))$$

can be represented as the following tree:

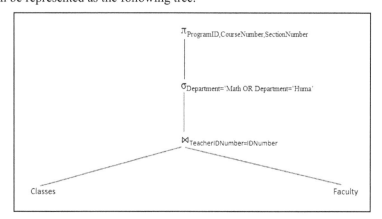

3.3.2.2 Tree Example 2

The computation of earlier example 3.3.1.2:

$$Personnel \bowtie_{Personnel.IDNumber=EnrolledIn.IDNumber}($$
$$\pi_{ProgramID,CourseNumber,SectionNumber,EnrolledIn.IDNumber}($$
$$EnrolledIn \bowtie (\sigma_{Gender='M'}(Classes \bowtie_{TeacherIDNumber=IDNumber} Personnel)$$
$$)$$
$$)$$
$$)$$

can be represented as the following tree:

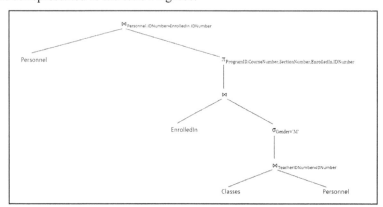

3.3.3 Alternative Representations

There is often more than one relational algebra expression that represents the same computation (i.e. that will produce the same relations.) This is one of the primary benefits of basing query languages on relational algebras. When we have several different equivalent expressions for evaluating a given computation, the computations using the different expressions will not (necessarily) be evaluated equally efficiently.

An important job of a query "optimizer" is to identify equivalent alternative expressions and determine which can be evaluated most efficiently

Example: The example in 3.3.1.1

$$\pi_{ProgramID,CourseNumber,SectionNumber}((\sigma_{Department='Math'}(Classes \bowtie_{TeacherIDNumber=IDNumber}Faculty)) \cup (\sigma_{Department='Huma'}(Classes \bowtie_{TeacherIDNumber=IDNumber}Faculty)))$$

could also be computed (possibly more efficiently) as:

$$\pi_{ProgramID,CourseNumber,SectionNumber}((\sigma_{Department='Math\ OR\ Department='Huma'}(Classes \bowtie_{TeacherIDNumber=IDNumber}Faculty)))$$

which would have the following tree representation

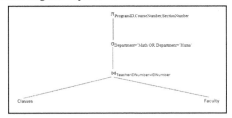

3.3.4 Renaming

It is often useful to use an operator that explicitly renames relations. We will use the symbol ρ to designate the renaming operator.

$\rho_S(R)$ will produce a relation named S, having the same attributes and tuples as R

$\rho_{S(A1, A2 \dots ,An)}(R)$ represents a relation named S, having the same tuples as R, but whose attributes have been renamed to A1, A2, ..., An

These attributes must have the same domains as the original attributes. (Note that the renaming operator IS dependent on the order of the attributes, and this *does* somewhat contradict what we said in 2.7.1)

3.3.4.1 Renaming Example

Recall that in our earlier examples attributes Classes.TeacherIDNumber and Faculty.IDNumber refer to the same entities.

The renaming operation

$\rho_{CLS(ProgramID, CourseNumber, SectionNumber, IDNumber, RoomID)}(Classes)$

would allow us to use the natural join CLS$\bowtie$Faculty rather than the theta join

$Classes \bowtie_{TeacherIDNumber=IDNumber}Faculty$

in our queries:

and, instead of the tree representation from 3.3.3, we might have the following form:

3.3.5 Linear/Sequential Notation for Algebraic Expressions

We can create an alternative technique for describing a query computation in tree format.

(a technique called *sequential assignment*)

We would do this by:

Creating names for each of the interior nodes of a tree representation.

Writing a sequence of assignment statements creating (computed) values for each of the invented names.

The order of these assignment statements is (generally) quite flexible.

3.3.5.1 Linear Notation Example

The computation described by the tree in 3.3.4.1 could be described by the following sequence of assignments:

$Cmp1 = \rho_{CLS(ProgramID, CourseNumber, SectionNumber, IDNumber, RoomID)}(Classes)$

$Cmp2 = Cmp1 \bowtie Faculty$

$Cmp3 = \sigma_{Department='Math' \; OR \; Department='Huma'}(Cmp2)$

$FinalResult = \pi_{ProgramID,CourseNumber,SectionNumber}(Cmp3)$

3.3.6 Constraints on Relations

Constraints place limitations/restrictions on the data that may be stored in the database

We have already encountered one common constraint, that of an attribute or collection of attributes being a *key*.

This kind of constraint can be specified in SQL by the declarations "PRIMARY KEY" or "UNIQUE"

There are many other types of constraints that can be expressed in relational algebra.

Another common type of constraint is the *referential integrity* constraint, a requirement that values appearing in a column of one relation also appear in a column of another relation.

3.3.6.1 Formats for Relational Algebra Constraints

There are two basic formats for expressing constraints in relational algebra

- If R is a relational algebra expression, then $R = \phi$ is a constraint

  The symbol ϕ represents the empty set so this constraint specifies that there be no tuples that satisfy the expression R

- If R and S are expressions, then $R \subseteq S$ is a constraint

  This constraint requires that any tuple satisfying condition R must also satisfy condition S (although there might be tuples satisfying S that do not satisfy R)

Any constraint described using one of these formats can also be described in the other (although in some cases one format might be more easily understood than the other.) [8]

The statement $R \subseteq S$ is equivalent to $R-S=\phi$ and $R=\phi$ could also be stated in the form $R\subseteq\phi$. (The $R=\phi$ format is the most commonly used in SQL.)

---

[8]   We note that the requirement that an attribute (or set of attributes) is a key *can* be expressed in the indicated format, but such an expression is likely to be very complex.

3.3.6.2 Referential Integrity Constraints

A *referential integrity* constraint asserts that a value appearing in one context also appears in another (related) context

In our "Classes" relation, we would certainly expect that a "TeacherIDNumber" value should also appear as an "IDNumber" value in one of the "Faculty" relation tuples and also in one of the "Personnel" tuples.

If our design intentions require that a particular value (attribute A) in one relation (relation R) must also appear as a value in another relation (relation S) as the value of an attribute (attribute B) then we can specify this requirement (constraint) as $\pi_A(R) \subseteq \pi_B(S)$

– or as $\pi_A(R) - \pi_B(S) = \phi$

3.3.6.2.1 Referential Integrity Constraint Example 1

The constraint that a "TeacherIDNumber" attribute value in relation "Classes" must be a value of the "IDNumber" attribute for some value in table "Faculty" could be expressed either as $\pi_{TeacherIDNumber}(Classes) \subseteq \pi_{IDNumber}(Faculty)$
or as $\pi_{TeacherIDNumber}(Classes) - \pi_{IDNumber}(Faculty) = \phi$

3.3.6.2.2 Referential Integrity Constraint Example 2

The constraint that a "IDNumber" attribute value in relation "EnrolledIn" must also be a "IDNumber" value in table "Student" could be expressed either as
$\pi_{IDNumber}(EnrolledIn) \subseteq \pi_{IDNumber}(Student)$
or as $\pi_{IDNumber}(EnrolledIn) - \pi_{IDNumber}(Student) = \phi$

3.3.6.3 Other Constraints

There are many other kinds of useful constraints that we can express using relational algebra. Many of these constraints involve the domains of attributes.

3.3.6.3.1 Domain Example

The restriction that "Gender" values in relation "Faculty" are restricted to 'M' and 'F' can be expressed as $\sigma_{Gender \neq 'F' \text{ AND } Gender \neq 'M'}(Faculty) = \phi$

3.4 Chapter 3 Questions:
  3.4.1 True-False
    3.4.1.1 Relational Algebra (like all algebras) allows us to form expressions of arbitrary complexity, by applying operations to results of other operations
    3.4.1.2 The requirement that an attribute (or set of attributes) is a key cannot be expressed algebraically
  3.4.2 Multiple Choice
    3.4.2.1 R∪S, the *union* of R and S, is
        a. the collection of elements that are in R, in S, or in both.
        b. the collection of all elements that are in *both* R *and* S
        c. the collection of elements that are in R but not in S
        d. the collection of elements that are in S but not in R
        e. none of the above

    3.4.2.2 R-S, the *difference* of R and S, is
        a. the collection of elements that are in R, in S, or in both.
        b. the collection of all elements that are in *both* R *and* S
        c. the collection of elements that are in R but not in S
        d. the collection of elements that are in S but not in R
        e. none of the above

    3.2.2.3 R ⋈$_C$ S represents the _____ join of R and S
        a. *C*
        b. theta
        c. natural
        d. complete
        e. none of the above

    3.2.2.4 $\sigma_C(R×S) =$
        a. the intersection of R and S
        b. the union of R and S
        c. the natural join of of R and S
        d. all of the above
        e. none of the above

  3.4.3 Completion
    3.4.3.1 In a database model, there must be operations to query and modify the data. At the base of querying and modifying data is a _____ *algebra*
    3.4.3.2 An algebra consists of _____ and operands
    3.4.3.3 We generally refer to expressions of relational algebra as _____
    3.5.3.4 The attribute set for the natural join of R and S is the _____ of the attribute sets for R and S
    3.4.3.5 _____ place limitations/restrictions on the data that may be stored in a database

Chapter 4 Design Theory for Relational Databases: Functional Dependencies

When we set out to design a database for a system of data, there will typically be many different schemas that we might use. Some designs will have advantages for representing and dealing with some kinds of applications and other designs will be better for other kinds of applications.

As an example, we have the option of representing data concerning college faculty as
Faculty(IDNumber:string, LastName:string, FirstName:string, Office:string, Phone:string, DeptID:string)
or as
Faculty(IDNumber:string, OfficeID:string, DeptID:string
Personnel(IDNumber:string, LastName:string, FirstName:string)
Offices(OfficeID:string, OfficePhone:string)

The first structure will involve fewer files for storing the data, but each faculty reference would involve more information, and so would take a little longer to process. More importantly, with this structure, if professors share an office (as is common) the office phone number will be stored in each Faculty entry. The same information (office phone number) will be stored in multiple locations, taking extra storage space and this creates the potential for inconsistency. If there were to be an update of office phone numbers, it would be possible that the record only one of the people in the office might be updated.

For a system of any complexity, the initial design attempt will (almost) certainly have room for (a great deal of) improvement.

In particular, an initial attempt is likely to include many redundancies. Storing the same information in more than one place is, of course, inefficient in terms of storage management, but (much worse) creates the potential for *inconsistencies* in the data stored in the database. Data updates might easily modify the values stored in one location and not those in another. As a result, a query utilizing one location could produce a different result than a query referencing the other.

Correct representation of information is the single most important factor for any database and with *inconsistent* data it is absolutely certain that at least one of the values is wrong.

Thus, in the process of "improving" an initial attempt for a schema, the elimination of (potential) redundancies is of primary concern.

4.1 Functional Dependencies

There is a well developed theory for designing relational databases, based on analyzing "dependencies".

This theory provides techniques for identifying and eliminating potential flaws. It lets us examine a design and identify problems and make improvements.

The technique begins with the *constraints* that apply to the relation.

The first type of constraint the technique deals with is that of being a "*functional dependency*".

Functional dependency is a generalization of the concept of being a *key* for a relation.

Design Theory for Relational Databases: Functional Dependencies

4.1.1 Functional Dependency: Definition

A *functional dependency* (FD) on a relation R is a statement of the form

"Two tuples that agree on all of the attributes A1, A2, ..., An must also agree on all attributes B1, B2, ..., Bm"

- We can describe this situation by writing:
  A1, A2, ..., An → B1, B2, ..., Bm

- We can also describe the situation in words, saying:
  A1, A2, ..., An *functionally determine* B1, B2, ..., Bm

If we can be sure that, in a relation R, an FD is true, then we say that R *satisfies* the FD.

4.1.1.1 Functional Dependencies: Commentary

When we say that R satisfies an FD, we are asserting a constraint on the *structure* of R, not a particular instance of R

It is common for the right side of an FD to be a single attribute

The FD A1, A2, ..., An → B1, B2, ..., Bm is equivalent to the *set* of FD's
A1, A2, ..., An → B1
A1, A2, ..., An → B2
....
A1, A2, ..., An → Bm

4.1.1.2 Functional Dependencies:Example

In the table below (identified as Classes):

As discussed in chapter 2, the combination of ProgramID, CourseNumber and SectionNumber identifies a specific class. The class will be assigned a classroom and have a specific teacher. We can say ProgramID, CourseNumber and SectionNumber *functionally determine* TeacherIDNumber and RoomID, or more succinctly:

ProgramID, CourseNumber, SectionNumber → TeacherIDNumber, RoomID

Classes				
ProgramID	CourseNumber	SectionNumber	TeacherIDNumber	RoomID
BIOL	2212	020	444917012	DUP311
COMP	1001	011	744500105	TUR203
MATH	3101	122	514067723	FUN101
SCLP	4123	161	888991121	HUM202

There might well be various classes with CourseNumber 1001 and Section 011 (possibly BIOL 1001 Section 011) but if an expanded Classes table were to include another tuple with ProgramID value COMP, CourseNumber value 1001 and SectionNumber 011, then in that tuple the TeacherIDNumber value in that tuple would also have to be 744500105 and the RoomID value would have to be TUR203.

However, no proper subcollection from {Program, Course, Section} functionally determines any of the other attributes.

Design Theory for Relational Databases: Functional Dependencies

4.1.2 Keys: Functional Dependency Definition

We can describe a set of one or more attributes {A1, … An} as being a *key* for the relation R if:

1. {A1, … An} functionally determines each of the remaining attributes.

2. No smaller subset of {A1, … An} functionally determines all other attributes.

   - In other words, the set {A1, … An} is *minimal* with respect to functionally determining all other attributes.

4.1.2.1 Our comments in 4.1.1.2 indicated that the set
        {ProgramID, CourseNumber, SectionNumber}
   is a *key* for the relation "Classes"

4.1.2.2 Sometimes a relation has more than one key.

If we were to have used the Personnel schema:

Personnel(
    IDNumber:string,
    SocSec:string
    LastName:string,
    FirstName:string,
    Gender:CHAR(1)
)

Personnel				
IDNumber	SocSec	LastName	FirstName	Gender
444917012	212325561	Smith	Samuel	M
614726215	655872435	Oatie	Donkey	M
514067723	774123571	Johnson	Robert	M
744150105	257553714	Watanabe	Kimberly	F
521788724	785247415	Avvoltoio	Victoria	F
601552112	335247864	Beamish	John	M
888991121	545336921	Hare	Harvey	M
801428821	623554503	Reller	Cindy	F
803526671	547219965	Lugo	Belinda	F
802465401	777953021	Panda	Sancho	M
801488722	696756968	Rabbit	Jack	M

then either IDNumber or SocSec could serve as a key.

When a relation has more than one key, it is common to designate one of the keys as the *primary key* for the relation.

In such a case, which key is chosen as primary key can influence some implementation issues, but the theory of FD's places no special role for *primary* keys.

53

Design Theory for Relational Databases: Functional Dependencies

4.1.3 Superkeys

We use the term *superkey* to describe a set of attributes that *contains* a key.

(In other words: a *superkey* is a *superset* of a key.)

A superkey satisfies the first condition for being a key (it functionally determines all remaining attributes) but a superkey does not (necessarily) satisfy the second condition (minimality.)

Note that *every* relation has at least one superkey.

The collection of *all* attributes of a relation R is *necessarily* a superkey for R.

4.2 Rules About Functional Dependencies

If we are told that a relation satisfies a given set of FD's, we can very often conclude that it also satisfies other FD's as well.

This ability (the ability to derive new FD's that a relation satisfies) is essential in the design of good relation schemes.

FD's can often be presented in different ways without changing the set of legal instances of the relation.

Two sets of FD's, S and T, are said to be *equivalent* if the set of relation instances satisfying S is exactly the same as the set of instances satisfying T.

A set S, of FD's, is said to *follow from* another set T, of FD's, if every relation instance that satisfies T must also satisfy S.

(This does not necessarily imply that every instance satisfying S also satisfies T.)

4.2.1 Reasoning About Functional Dependencies: Example:

In a relation R(A,B,C), if we know A→B and B→C then we can conclude A→C .

{A→C} *follows from* { A→B, B→C}

To establish that this is true, consider two tuples (a1,b1,c1) and (a2,b2,c2). If a1=a2 then, since A→B, we know b1=b2. Now, since B→C and b1=b2 we can conclude c1=c2. Hence, if a1=a2 then c1=c2, and, thus, A→C.

4.2.2 Rules About Functional Dependencies: The Splitting/Combining Rule

We have already noted that A1, A2, ..., An → B1, B2, ..., Bm is equivalent to the set of FD's
A1, A2, ..., An → B1
A1, A2, ..., An → B2,
....
A1, A2, ..., An → Bm

This says we may *split* an FD of the form A1, A2, ..., An → B1, B2, ..., Bm into several simpler FD's (each having only one attribute on the right hand side.)

There is no corresponding splitting rule for left sides.

The *splitting rule* also says we can combine certain kinds of collections of several FD's into single (albeit more complex) FD's.

Design Theory for Relational Databases: Functional Dependencies

4.2.3 Rules About Functional Dependencies: Trivial Functional Dependencies

A constraint C on a relation R is said to be *trivial* if every possible instance of R satisfies C

(i.e. does not *constrain* anything.)

For constraints in the form of FD's, the trivial constraints are easy to identify.

They are the FD's of the form:
A1, A2, ..., An → B1, B2, ..., Bm where
{B1, B2, ..., Bm} ⊆ {A1, A2, ..., An}

Such a constraint places no restrictions on the relation.

Any tuple in *any* instance of R will assign specific values for each Ai, but each Bj is Ak for some k, and, so, must have already been assigned a specific value.

4.2.3.1 Rules About Trivial Functional Dependencies

If SOME, but not all, of the attributes on the right side of an FD are contained in the left side

A1, A2,.., An, B1, B2,., Bm → B1, B2,., Bm, C1, C2,... Ck

then this FD is equivalent to the FD obtained by removing from the right side, those attributes that appear on the left side

A1, A2, ..., An, B1, B2, ..., Bm→ C1, C2, ... Ck

This, of course, results in a simpler constraint.

4.2.4 Rules About Functional Dependencies: The Closure of a Set of Attributes

For any relation R, any set A= {A1, A2, ..., An} of attributes of R, and any collection S of FD's involving attributes of R, the *closure under S of A* is the collection {B1, B2, ..., Bm} of all attributes Bi of R such that every instance of R which satisfies all FD's in S, also satisfies the FD A1, A2, ..., An → Bi

This closure is designated A+ or {A1, A2, ..., An}+

Note that {A1, A2, ..., An} ⊆ {A1, A2, ..., An}+

- This must be true because A1, A2, ..., An → Ai is always trivial.

4.2.4.1 Algorithm for Computing the Closure of Attributes:

Input: Set {A1, A2, ..., An} of attributes and set S of FD's

Output: {A1, A2, ..., An}+

1. Split the collection S into FD's with single attributes on right sides

2. Initialize set X = {A1, A2, ..., An}

3. Repeat

if for some attribute C in R not already in X, it is true that X → C

then X:= X∪{C}

until no such attribute exists

4. Output X as {A1, A2, ..., An}+

4.2.4.2 Example of Application of the Algorithm

Consider a relation with attributes A, B, C, D, E, F
and with FD's {AB → C, BC → AD, D→E, CF→B}

To find {A,B}+
   1. (Split the FD's) S = {AB → C, BC → A, BC → D, D→E, CF→B}
   2. (Initialize X) X = {A,B}
   3. AB→C from FD #1 in S so X := {A,B,C}
       A,B,C→D from FD #3 in S so X := {A,B,C,D}
       A,B,C,D→E from FD #4 in S so X := {A,B,C,D,E}
       there is no FD in S with F on right side so F is NOT in {A,B}+ ,
       hence {A,B}+ = {A,B,C,D,E}

4.2.5 Why the Algorithm Works

In order to prove that this algorithm "works" we must show two things

   1.   If B is a member of {A1, A2, ..., An}+ (as computed by the algorithm)
        then A1, A2, ..., An → B in every relation instance satisfying S

   2.   If A1, A2, ..., An → B in every relation instance satisfying S,
        then B is a member of {A1, A2, ..., An}+ (as computed by the algorithm)

4.2.5.1 Why the Algorithm Works #1

The set {A1, A2, ..., An}+ is computed in a sequence of steps.

If B∈X initially, in step 0, then B = Ai for some i and so {A1, A2, ..., An} → B
trivially in every relation instance satisfying S

Suppose, then, that at step k, X := {A1, A2, ..., An, B1, B2, ..., Bk}
and that A1, A2, ..., An → B1, B2, ..., Bk in every relation satisfying S.

In the next step (step k+1), the attribute added is an attribute C such that X → C for
each relation instance satisfying S.

For any two tuples in a relation instance satisfying S, if the two tuples agree on
{A1, A2, ..., An} then they must also agree on B1, ..., Bk and so must agree on
A1, A2, ..., An, B1, B2, ..., Bk and, hence must agree on attribute C as well.

Therefore A1, A2, ..., An → C

4.2.5.2 Why the Algorithm Works #2

To show #2, simply consider an attribute C which is not in {A1, A2, ..., An}+

After the last step in the computation, there were no attributes D left for which
A1, A2, ..., An → D in every relation instance satisfying S. (If there were another such
attribute D, there would have been another step.)

Therefore it cannot be true that A1, A2, ..., An→ C.

Design Theory for Relational Databases: Functional Dependencies

4.2.6 The Transitive Rule

Another rule that holds for FD's is the *transitive rule*.

The *transitive rule* says that in a relation R,
 if A1, A2, ..., An → B1, B2, ..., Bm
 and if B1, B2, ..., Bm → C1, C2, ..., Cp
 then A1, A2, ..., An → C1, C2, ..., Cp

To see that this is true, consider two tuples that agree on {A1,A2, ...,An}

 – Since A1, A2, ..., An → B1, B2, ..., Bm they must also agree on {B1,B2, ...,Bm}

 – Then, since B1, B2, ..., Bm → C1, C2, ..., Cp they must also agree on {C1,C2, ...,Cp}

4.2.7 Bases for sets of FDs

If we are given a set S of FD's

(We will most commonly be interested in the collection of ALL FD's that hold in a given relation, but this will not always be the case.)

then any set of FD's equivalent to S is said to be a *basis* for S

A *minimal* basis for a relation S is a basis B for S such that:

1. Every FD in B has a single attribute on the right side.

2. If any FD is removed from B, the remaining set is not a basis for S.

3. If, in any FD in B, one or more attributes is removed from the left side, the resulting set is not a basis for S.

4.2.7.1 Example

Consider a relation R(A,B,C) and suppose we know that in this relation each attribute functionally determines each other attribute.

This says that the complete set of FD's for this relation *includes* the FD's

 A → B, A → C, B → A, B → C, C → A, C → B

The complete set of FD's on R will also include (in addition to numerous trivial dependencies) the collection: AB → C, AC → B, BC → A, A → BC B → AC and C → AB

The complete set of FD's on R has several minimal bases, including:

 {A → B, B → A, B → C, C → B}

 {A → B, B → C, C → A}

Design Theory for Relational Databases: Functional Dependencies

4.2.8 Projecting Functional Dependencies

When studying relations, it is common to be interested in only a limited set of attributes.

We would want to compute/identify what might be called "*subrelations*"

Suppose we have a relation R with a set S of FD's and that L is a subset of the attributes of R. Then we can define the projection R1 = $\pi_L(R)$

This raises the question, what FD's hold in R1

The answer is "all FD's in R that follow from FD's in S but involve only attributes in L"

Unfortunately, there will generally be MANY such FD's (and many of them will be redundant. That is, they follow from other such FD's)

In general, the computation involved in identifying these FD's will be exponential in the number of attributes in R1.

4.2.8.1 Dependencies: An algorithm for calculating the functional dependencies in a "subrelation"

INPUT: A relation R, a set S of FD's that hold in R, and L, a subset of the attributes of R

(i.e. $L \subseteq R$)

OUTPUT: The set T of FD's that hold in R1 = $\pi_L(R)$ resulting from S

Set T = ϕ

For each $X \subseteq L$,

compute X+ in R,

add each FD in X+ of the form X→A, with $A \in L$ to T

This creates a set T which is a basis for the FD's that hold in R1.

The set T, however, will (probably) not be a *minimal* basis.

In order to convert T into a minimal basis, we can proceed as follows:

Repeat

If there is some F, an FD in T, that follows from the other FD's in T, then remove F from T.

For each FD in T of the form Y → B with Y having two or more attributes

If, for any attribute y in Y, if Z→B follows from the FD's in T,
where Z=Y-{y}
replace Y→B by Z→B

Until neither of the above can be performed.

4.2.8.2 Example of the application of the algorithm

Suppose FD's A→B, B→C, C→D hold in a relation R(A,B,C,D) and we wish to compute the FD's that hold in the projection R1(A,C,D)

To compute these FD's, our algorithm says to first compute the closures of all subsets of {A,C,D}

The empty set Φ and the entire set {A,C,D} can yield only trivial FD's so we consider only the closures of the sets {A}, {C}, {D}, {AC}, {AD}, and {C,D}

T=φ

{A}+ = {A,B,C,D}

   T ={A→C, A→D}

{C}+ = {C,D}

   T ={A→C, A→D, C →D}

{D}+ = {D}, so we can add no nontrivial FD's

Since {A}+ = {A,B,C,D}, any FD with left side AC or AD would be trivial

{C,D}+ = {C,D}, and, again no nontrivial FD's can be added

Now we have that T ={A→C, A→D,C→D} is a basis for the FD's in R1.

But T is not minimal, since A→D follows from A→C and C→D.

T ={A→C, C→D} however, is a minimal basis for the FD's in R1

4.3 Design of Relational Databases

Lack of care in the design of a database can lead to redundancy and anomalies.

In the table below (called FacultyWithPhone), the values for OfficeID and OfficePhone are repeated for two of the professors.

FacultyWithPhone			
IDNumber	OfficeID	DeptID	OfficePhone
444917012	DUP409	Scie	3434
614726215	DUP411	Scie	3481
514067723	MTH323	Math	6552
744150105	TUR411	Math	3921
521788724	DUP510	Scie	3460
601552112	FOR403	Lang	6323
888991121	HUM504	Huma	5223
703333215	DUP409	Scie	3434
512459758	MTH323	Math	6552

The OfficePhone values in fact depend on the DeptID values so the repetition of the OfficePhone values would result in an inefficient use of storage, but, much worse, it would also introduce the potential for several kinds of *anomalies*.

Design Theory for Relational Databases: Functional Dependencies

4.3.1 Anomalies

One of the most common kinds of *anomaly* that we encounter in database design is *redundancy*:

information repeated unnecessarily, appearing in more than one tuple

Redundancies create the potential for one of the worst kind of problems that can exist in a database, inconsistent data:

Inconsistent data (given redundant structures in the database) will often be due to improper update procedures.

- *Update anomalies*: These occur if we change information in one tuple and fail to make the corresponding change in another tuple.

  - If our example college (FacultyWithPhone example from section 4.3 above) were to upgrade their telephone system and, in the process, were to decide to change the phone number in office DUP409 to 3575 they might easily update the OfficePhone attribute for the professor with ID 444917012, but forget to update the number of professor with ID 703333215, This would result in different phone numbers listed for office DUP409 *-inconsistent* data in the database–

Inconsistent information is not the only kind of problem that can occur in a database. Another type of problem is that of the inadvertent deletion of information.

  Deletion anomalies: If a set of values is deleted, the process might result in the loss of other information as well

  - As the FacultyWithPhone relation is structured, removal of the record for professor 614726215 from the table would eliminate the record of the information that phone number 3481 assigned to office DUP411.

4.3.2 Decomposing Relations

The accepted way of eliminating these kinds of anomalies is to *decompose* the relations.

- *Decomposition* of a relation R, involves *splitting* the attributes of R to make schemas of two new relations

- Given a relation R(A1,...,An), we may decompose R into two relations S(B1,...Bm) and T(C1,...,Ck) with

  - $\{A1,...,An\}=\{B1,...Bm\} \cup \{C1,...,Ck\}$

  - $S = \pi_{B1,...Bm}(R)$

  - $T = \pi_{C1,...,Ck}(R)$

Design Theory for Relational Databases: Functional Dependencies

4.3.2.1 Decomposing Relations: Example

We can decompose the above "FacultyWithPhone" relation into:

- A relation Faculty, whose schema has attributes IDNumber, OfficeID, and DeptID

- A relation Offices, whose schema has attributes OfficeID and OfficePhone

The projection of "FacultyWithPhone" onto these two new schemas is shown below

Faculty				Offices	
IDNumber	OfficeID	DeptID		OfficeID	OfficePhone
444917012	DUP409	Scie		DUP409	3434
614726215	DUP411	Scie		DUP411	3481
514067723	MTH323	Math		MTH323	6552
744150105	TUR411	Math		TUR411	3921
521788724	DUP510	Scie		DUP510	3460
601552112	FOR403	Lang		FOR403	6323
888991121	HUM504	Huma		HUM504	5223
703333215	DUP409	Scie			
512459758	MTH323	Math			

- This decomposition reduces the risk of update anomalies by eliminating the redundant values of "OfficePhone" in "FacultyWithPhone".

  - If we to were change the phone number for office DUP409, as there is only one tuple with this value, the number cannot be listed with two different values, as it could with the "FacultyWithPhone" schema.

- The risk of deletion anomalies is also reduced

  - If the entry for prof 614726215 is removed from the Faculty table, the phone number for office DUP411is still available in the database in table Offices.

Design Theory for Relational Databases: Functional Dependencies

4.4 Chapter 4 Questions:

4.4.1 True-False

4.4.1.1 It is common for an initial relational schema to have room for improvement

4.4.1.2 A "functional dependency" is a statement of a type generalizing the idea of a *key* for a relation

4.4.1.3 Most relations do not have superkeys

4.4.1.4 A set of FD's S is said to *follow from* a set of FD's T if every relation instance that satisfies T must also satisfy S

4.4.1.5 The splitting/combining rule says we may *split* an FD of the form
$A_1, A_2, ..., A_n ? B_1, B_2, ..., B_m$
into several simpler FD's (having only one attribute on the right hand side)

4.4.1.6 An FD of the form $AB \rightarrow BC$
is equivalent to $AB \rightarrow C$

4.4.1.7 *redundancy* is an inefficient use of storage, but, much worse, it introduces the potential for several kinds of errors

4.4.2 Multiple Choice

4.4.2.1 A principal kind of anomaly that we encounter in database design is:

   a. redundancy
   b. update anomaly
   c. deletion anomaly
   d. all of the above
   e. none of the above

4.4.3 Completion

4.4.3.1 It is common for an initial relational schema to have room for improvement
   – Especially by removing _____

4.4.3.2 We say that a set of one or more attributes, $\{A_1, ... A_n\}$, is a (n) _____ for the relation R if:
   • $\{A_1, ... A_n\}$ functionally determines each of the remaining attributes
   • No smaller subset of $\{A_1, ... A_n\}$ functionally determines all other attributes

4.4.3.3 A constraint C on a relation R is said to be _____ if every instance of R satisfies C

4.4.3.4 Suppose we have a relation R with a set of FD's S. If L is a subset of R, then we can define the _____ to be $R_1 = \pi_L(R)$.

4.4.3.5 Lack of care in the design of a database can lead to redundancy and _____

4.4.3.6 An accepted way of eliminating anomalies is to _____ the relations

Design Theory for Relational Databases: Normal Forms

Chapter 5 Design Theory for Relational Databases: Normal Forms

The goal of decomposition is to replace a single relation which has some anomalies with a collection of several relations that form a system with no anomalies.

There is a simple condition to determine whether a relation has any of the principal types of anomalies.

This condition is called the *Boyce-Codd normal form* (BCNF)

5.1 Design of Relational Databases Boyce-Codd Normal Form

A relation R is in BCNF if, whenever there is a nontrivial FD $A_1,...,A_n \rightarrow B_1,...,B_m$ the collection $\{A_1,...,A_n\}$ must be a superkey for R

- i.e. the left side of every nontrivial FD contains a key.

5.1.1 Boyce-Codd Normal Form: Example

The relation "FacultyWithPhone" (at the right) is NOT in BCNF

    OfficeID $\rightarrow$ OfficePhone is a nontrivial FD

but OfficeID would not functionally determine IDNumber and would not be a superkey for the relation.

FacultyWithPhone			
IDNumber	OfficeID	DeptID	OfficePhone
444917012	DUP409	Scie	3434
614726215	DUP411	Scie	3481
514067723	MTH323	Math	6552
744150105	TUR411	Math	3921
521788724	DUP510	Scie	3460
601552112	FOR403	Lang	6323
888991121	HUM504	Huma	5223
703333215	DUP409	Scie	3434
512459758	MTH323	Math	6552

5.1.2 Boyce-Codd Normal Form: Relations with Two Attributes

It will not always be obvious whether a relation is in BCNF, but one situation is very simple: Any relation with only two attributes must be in BCNF.

We can see this by considering four cases of a relation with two attributes R(A,B):

- The relation has no nontrivial FD's

  » For R NOT to be in BCNF, there must be a nontrivial FD whose left side is not a superkey. Since there are no nontrivial FD's, this cannot be the case, so R would be in BCNF.

- A→B holds but not B→A.

  » A is a key and any nontrivial FD must have A on left side.

- B→A holds but not A→B.

  » B is a key and any nontrivial FD must have B on left side

- Both A→B and B→A hold

  » A is a key and B is a key. Any nontrivial FD must have at least one of the two on the left side

Design Theory for Relational Databases: Normal Forms

5.1.3 Decomposition into BCNF

By repeatedly choosing suitable decompositions, we can subdivide any relation into a collection of subsets of its attributes such that:

– These subsets are schemas of relations in BCNF

– The data in the original relation is "represented *faithfully*"

(generally, this means all the original data can be recovered correctly from these subsets.)

5.1.3.1 BCNF Decomposition Algorithm

Our decomposition algorithm proceeds as follows:

– For a relation R(A1,...,An, B1,...,Bm , C1,...,Ck)

– Find a nontrivial FD A1,...,An → B1,...,Bm for which the collection {A1,...,An} is not a superkey

  • We will assume that the collection {B1,...,Bm} contains all attributes functionally determined by {A1,...,An}

– Divide R into two relations S(A1,...,An, B1,...,Bm) and T(A1,...,An, C1,...,Ck)

  • The resulting relations, S and T may not be in BCNF, but they have fewer attributes than R, and repeating the process must eventually result in relations that are in BCNF (recall that every relation with two attributes is in BCNF)

5.1.3.2 Decomposition into BCNF: Example

Suppose R(A,B,C,D,E) is a relation with FD's

A,B →C

C→D

D→E

The only key for R is {A, B}.

Each of the FD's C→D and D→E violate BCNF.

The FD C →D,E satisfies the conditions of the algorithm, so we divide R(A,B,C,D,E) into into R1(A,B,C) and R2(C,D,E)

R1 satisfies BCNF but R2 does not since D→E is a nontrivial FD and {D} is not a superkey.

R2 then, can be decomposed into R3(C,D) and R4(D,E)

This, then gives us a decomposition of R(A,B,C,D,E) into R1(A,B,C), R3(C,D) and R4(D,E), all three of which are BCNF relations.

Design Theory for Relational Databases: Normal Forms

5.1.4 Benefits of and Problems involved in Decompositions

A relation can have serious anomalies, and decomposition will eliminate these anomalies.

– That is good.

Unfortunately, this kind of decomposition can also result in "not so good" consequences

Desirable properties for decompositions would include:
1. Elimination of anomalies
2. Recoverability of information
3. Preservation of dependencies

We have just noted that decompositions carried out using the algorithm described earlier will always provide property #1. They will, in fact, also provide property #2. They will not, however, necessarily provide property #3

5.1.4.1 Recovering Information from a Decomposition

If it is possible to obtain all of the information in a relation from a decomposition, then the decomposition is called a *lossless join*.

If a decomposition is done according to the algorithm described earlier, then the projections of the original tuples can be joined again to produce all of the original tuples and only the original tuples.

We use a simplified situation with R(A,B,C) and an FD $B \rightarrow C$ to illustrate how, when the decomposition is done according to the algorithm, information can be recovered.

$B \rightarrow C$ is a BCNF violation.

The decomposition based on $B \rightarrow C$ is S(A,B) and T(B,C)

Suppose t = (a,b,c) is a tuple in R

The tuple t projects onto (a,b) in S and (b,c) in T

The natural join of (a,b) and (b,c) is (a,b,c) = t

Suppose, now, that (a,b,c) is in the join of S and T.

(a,b) is in S, so (a,b,d) is in R for some d.

(b,c) is in T, so (e,b,c) is in R for some e.

Since R satisfies $B \rightarrow C$, d must be equal to c, and so (a,b,c) is in R

The same type of argument works equally well if A, B and C are disjoint subsets of an attribute set for a relation, rather than single attributes. Hence, we can conclude that if a relation is decomposed according to our algorithm, all of the information can be recovered faithfully by the natural join.

We might note that at each step the decomposition algorithm uses FD $B \rightarrow C$ to divide the attributes of relation R, into three disjoint subsets, A, B, and C and establishes two relations, the projections S(A,B) and T(B,C) of R. It is because of the FD $B \rightarrow C$ that the relation R can be recovered as the natural join of S and T.

If, however, neither $B \rightarrow C$ nor $B \rightarrow A$, then the join of projections S(A,B) and T(B,C) will generally be able to include tuples that were not in R.

Design Theory for Relational Databases: Normal Forms

5.1.4.2 Lossless Joins

We have just seen that if we choose a decomposition correctly (according to the algorithm), then it will be a lossless join.

We now consider the problem of determining whether a given decomposition is, in fact, a lossless join.

Given a decomposition S1, S2, ..., Sn of the attributes of a relation R:

Is the join of the projections $\pi_{S1}(R) \bowtie \pi_{S2}(R) \bowtie ... \bowtie \pi_{Sn}(R)$ In fact equal to R?

Were the components chosen correctly?

There are three useful facts we can use in analyzing the join $\pi_{S1}(R) \bowtie \pi_{S2}(R) \bowtie ... \bowtie \pi_{Sn}(R)$

The natural join is associative and commutative.

(In whatever order we join the projections, we will get the same result)

The result of the join is a set of tuples t, such that for each j, the projection of t onto the set of attributes Sj is a tuple in $\pi_{Sj}(R)$

Any tuple t in R is in the join $\pi_{S1}(R) \bowtie \pi_{S2}(R) \bowtie ... \bowtie \pi_{Sn}(R)$ because for each j, the projection of t onto Sj is certainly in $\pi_{Sj}(R)$ and therefore t will be in the join

Therefore, $R \subseteq \pi_{S1}(R) \bowtie \pi_{S2}(R) \bowtie ... \bowtie \pi_{Sn}(R)$ and equality will hold, provided that every tuple in the join is also in R.

5.1.4.3 The Chase Test for Lossless Join

What is called the "*chase test for lossless joins*" provides an organized way, for using the FD's to determine whether every tuple in a natural join $\pi_{S1}(R) \bowtie \pi_{S2}(R) \bowtie ... \bowtie \pi_{Sn}(R)$ is also in the original relation R.

If a tuple t is in the join, there must be tuples t1, ... , tn in R such that t is the join of the projections $\pi_{Sj}(tj)$

We know that each tj agrees with t on entries in Sj but we do not know its projected values are for other attributes.

We draw a "picture" (called a tableau) illustrating what we know, putting subscripts on unknown values.

Next, we apply the FD's to attempt to reduce the number of unknown values in the tableau.

(We can identify the unknown values since they are the ones with subscripts.)

If, as we apply FD's, we discover that a row has no subscripted entries, then that row identifies the entries in a tuple from R which is the join of entries in the natural join $\pi_{S1}(R) \bowtie \pi_{S2}(R) \bowtie ... \bowtie \pi_{Sn}(R)$

In applying an FD, we might find that two entries must be equal. If one is unsubscripted, then that value must be substituted for the other. If both are subscripted, then either could be substituted for the other. (When a value is substituted, it must be substituted for all copies of the other.)

Design Theory for Relational Databases: Normal Forms

5.1.4.3.1 The Chase Test for Lossless Join: Example 1

Suppose a relation R(A,B,C,D) has FD's: $A \rightarrow B$, $B \rightarrow C$ and $CD \rightarrow A$ and has been decomposed into S1(A,D), S2(A,C), and S3(B,C,D)

Assuming that (a,b,c,d) is an element of the product $S1 \bowtie S2 \bowtie S3$

There is some t1 in R such that $\pi_{R1}(t1) = (a,d)$

t1 = (a,b1,c1,d) for some b1 and c1

There is some t2 in R such that $\pi_{R2}(t2) = (a,c)$

t2 = (a,b2,c,d2) for some b2 and d2

There is some t3 in R such that $\pi_{R3}(t3) = (b,c,d)$

t3 = (a3,b,c,d) for some a3

The tableau for this decomposition would look like Tableau#1:

A	B	C	D
a	b_1	c_1	d
a	b_2	c	d_2
a_3	b	c	d

Tableau#1

Since, in our tableau, the first two rows agree in their A components, the FD A→B requires that they also agree in their B components.

This creates Tableau#2

A	B	C	D
a	b_1	c_1	d
a	b_1	c	d_2
a_3	b	c	d

Tableau#2

In Tableau#2, the first two rows agree in their B component.

The FD $B \rightarrow C$ gives us Tableau#3

A	B	C	D
a	b_1	c	d
a	b_1	c	d_2
a_3	b	c	d

Tableau#3

In Tableau#3, rows 1 and 3 agree in the C and D components, and so the FD $CD \rightarrow A$ tells us that they should agree in the A component.

This gives us Tableau#4.

A	B	C	D
a	b_1	c	d
a	b_1	c	d_2
a	b	c	d

Tableau#4

Since in row 3 of Tableau#4, none of the entries have subscripts, we can conclude that the decomposition is a lossless join.

5.1.4.3.2 Why the Chase Works

First, if the process results in an entry with no subscripts, then that entry must, in fact, be the tuple t produced by the join.

If, on the other hand, after we have reached a tableau in which no more FD's can be applied, no such row exists, then, the resulting tableau would constitute an instance of a relation R which does not include tuple t. We can project *this* relation onto the components and the natural join does include the tuple t.

5.1.4.3.3 The Chase Test: Example 2

Consider relation R(A,B,C,D) with FD
B→AD and decomposition {A,B},
{B,C} and {C,D}

The initial tableau would look like
Tableau#5

A	B	C	D
a	b	c_1	d_1
a_2	b	c	d_2
a_3	b_3	c	d

Tableau#5

From the FD B→AD, we can conclude
$a_2 = a$ and $d_1 = d_2$

This gives us Tableau#6

A	B	C	D
a	b	c_1	d_1
a	b	c	d_1
a_3	b_3	c	d

Tableau#6

Tableau#6 is in final form, since the only FD (B→AD) can produce no more changes.

No row is fully unsubscripted, so the chase algorithm tells us that the decomposition does not have a lossless join.

As a relation, Tableau#6 satisfies the FD and the projections:

onto {A,B} is {(a,b), (a3,b3)}

onto {B,C} is {(b,c1), (b,c), {b3,c)}

onto {C,D} is {(c1,d1), (c,d1),(c,d)}

We observe, now, that (a,b,c,d) is a member of the natural join of these three relations, but is not a member of the original relation.

5.1.4.2 Dependency Preservation

We mentioned earlier that, in some cases, it is not (always) possible to decompose a relation into BCNF relations that are both lossless and dependency preserving:

5.1.4.2.1 Example

Suppose our campus has several different libraries and that the libraries all store their books in different "archives".

Consider a relation Books(Isbn, Library, Archive)

"Isbn" is the identification code used to identify books.

"Library" is the name of library building on the campus.

"Archive" identifies where a collection of books is stored (usually books related to a specific discipline.)

Design Theory for Relational Databases: Normal Forms

The intent of a tuple (I,L,A) in relation "Books" would be to record that a copy of a book identified by Isbn code I would be found stored in archive A in library L.

It seems reasonable that the following FD's would hold for the relation Books

Archive→Library

Isbn Library→Archive

In this relation, no single attribute is a key.

{Isbn, Library} is a key because of FD Isbn Library→Archive

{Archive, Isbn} is also a key because of FD Archive→Library

{Archive, Library} however, do not functionally determine Isbn because a given archive in a given library will typically have many different books.

There is an obvious BCNF violation in this relation:

Archive→Library is an FD but {Archive} is not a superkey

According to the algorithm, we would deal with this violation by decomposing the Books relation into:

AL(Archive,Library) and AI(Archive,Isbn)

This decomposition, however, does not support the FD Isbn Library→Archive

The tuples (Physics, FoundersLibrary) and (Math, FoundersLibrary) are legitimate entries for AL

The tuples:
(Physics, 9781091725072)
and (Math, 9781091725072)
are legitimate entries for AI

However, the combinations
(Physics,FoundersLibrary,9781091725072)
and (Math,FoundersLibrary, 9781091725072)
violate the FD Isbn Library→Archive

5.2 Third Normal Form

The solution to the problem illustrated by the previous example is to create a slightly less restrictive condition than BCNF

This relaxed condition is called the "third normal form" or 3NF

(There are several other "normal forms")

First normal form (1NF) is the requirement that all components be atomic values

Second normal form (2NF) is a less restrictive version of 3NF and is seldom referred to outside of theoretical treatments of database analysis.

There is also a 4NF and we will cover that normal form shortly.

Design Theory for Relational Databases: Normal Forms

5.2.1 Third Normal Form Definition

A relation R is in third normal form (3NF) if:

for any nontrivial FD A1, ... , An → B1, ... , Bm in R, either {A1, ... , An} is a superkey or each of the members Bi that are not in {A1, ... , An} are in some key (not necessarily all in the same key.)

An attribute that is a member of a key is sometimes said to be *prime* and, with this terminology, we can phrase the definition of 3NF as:

For any nontrivial FD A1, ... , An → B1, ... , Bm

either {A1, ... , An} is a superkey

or each Bi not in {A1, ... , An} must be prime.

5.2.2 Third Normal Form Synthesis Algorithm

The objective of 3NF decomposition of a relation R is to create a set of subrelations such that

The subrelations are all in 3NF

The natural join of the subrelations forms a lossless join decomposition of R

The decomposition preserves dependencies

INPUT: A relation R and a set F of functional dependencies that hold for R

OUTPUT: A decomposition of R into a collection of relations, each in 3NF, the decomposition having lossless-join and dependency-preservation properties

METHOD: Perform the following:

1. Find a minimal basis G for F

2. For each FD X→A in G, use XA as the schema for a relation in the decomposition

3. If none of the schemas from step 2 is a superkey for R, then add another relation whose schema is a key for R

5.2.2.1 Third Normal Form Decomposition Example[i]

Consider the relation R(A,B,C,D,E) with FD's AB→C, C→B, and A→D

This set of FD's is, in fact, a minimal basis (not easy to show, but, trust us, it *is* minimal.)

We start the process by taking attribute sets S1(A,B,C), S2(B,C) and S3(A,D)

Since {B,C} is a subset of {A,B,C} we can drop S2.

None of the sets involve attribute E, so none is a superkey for R. The keys for R are {A,B,E} and {A,C,E}, so we add another relation, S4, using one of them, say S4(A,B,E)

Then, S1, S3 and S4 form a decomposition of R. All three will be in 3NF and the decomposition will be lossless and dependency preserving.

Design Theory for Relational Databases: Normal Forms

5.2.2.2 Why the 3NF Synthesis Algorithm Works:

Lossless Join

Suppose R1 is a relation from the decomposition and that the set K, of attributes for R1 is a superkey.

Consider the sequence of FD's that expand K to K+

Since K is a superkey, we know that K+ consists of all the attributes of R.

The same sequence of FD's, when applied to the tableau, will cause the subscripted symbols in the row corresponding to K to be equated to unsubscripted symbols, as attributes are added to the closure.

The chase test, then, will show that the decomposition is lossless.

Dependency Preservation:

Each FD in the minimal basis has all its attributes in some relation in the decomposition. Therefore each dependency can be checked in a decomposed relation

Third Normal Form: Showing that the relations must be in 3NF is beyond the scope of what we want to cover in this text. (You will just have to trust us that they are in 3NF.)

5.3 Multivalued Dependencies

A "multivalued dependency" (MVD) is an assertion that two attributes, or sets of attributes, are independent of one another.

This is a generalization of "functional dependency"

Every FD implies an MVD, but there are situations involving independence that cannot be explained as FD's

5.3.1 Multivalued Dependency: Example

We can assume that some (probably most) students have more than one parent, (who might or might not have divorced and remarried, which could result in students having even *more than* two official parents.) The school might consider, for their database, a relation with (partial) instance like that below:

StudentClassParent					
StudentID	Program	Course	Section	ParentLastName	ParentFirstName
...	...	...	...	...	...
712318791	COMP	1001	101	Morningside	Paul
712318791	MATH	1011	31	Morningside	Paul
712318791	COMP	1001	101	Stewart	Mary
712318791	MATH	1011	31	Stewart	Mary
...	...	...	...	...	...

Design Theory for Relational Databases: Normal Forms

There is clearly a great deal of redundancy in the "StudentClassParent" table, but there is no BCNF violation

There are, in fact, NO nontrivial FD's

The only key is the collection of all the attributes:
{StudentID, Program, Course, Section, ParentLastName, ParentFirstName}

5.3.2 Multivalued Dependency: Definition

A multivalued dependency (MVD) is a statement about some relation R requiring that, for a fixed collection of values of one set of attributes, the values of some other attributes are *independent* of the values in all the other attributes

– The MVD $A_1,\ldots,A_n \twoheadrightarrow B_1,\ldots,B_m$ holds for R if when we restrict ourselves to tuples of R that have specific values for each of the attributes $A_1,\ldots,A_n$, then the set of values among the B's is *independent* of attributes of R not among the A's or B's

More precisely, we can say that the MVD $A_1,\ldots,A_n \twoheadrightarrow B_1,\ldots,B_m$ holds if for each pair of tuples t and u in R that agree on $A_1,\ldots,A_n$ we can find some tuple v that agrees:

1. With t and u on $A_1,\ldots,A_n$

2. With t on $B_1,\ldots,B_m$

3. With u on all attributes of $R - \{A_1,\ldots,A_n,B_1,\ldots,B_m\}$

5.3.3 Multivalued Dependency: Example

In the example from 5.3.1 (relation StudentClassParent) we would have MVD StudentID$\twoheadrightarrow$ProgramCourseSection

Given two tuples t and u that agree on attribute StudentID (i.e. are tuples referring to the same student)

If t and u agree on Program, Course and Section then there is a tuple v that agrees with u on StudentID and with t on all other attributes. (That tuple is u itself.)

Suppose, then, that t and u do not agree on Program,Course,Section. Since the classes in which he/she enrolled have no effect on who the student's parents are, there is a tuple v which agrees with t on Program, Course and Section (The student IS enrolled in that class) and with u on ParentLastName and ParentFirstName because he/she is still the student's parent.

Design Theory for Relational Databases: Normal Forms

5.3.4 Multivalued Dependencies: Reasoning About MVD's

A number of MVD properties are similar to FD properties

Trivial MVD's

If B1,...,Bm ⊆ A1,...,An then A1,...,An ↠ B1,...,Bm

Transitive Rule

If A1, A2, ..., An ↠ B1, B2, ..., Bm and if B1, B2, ..., Bm ↠ C1, C2, ..., Cp
then A1, A2, ..., An ↠ C1, C2, ..., Cp and any C's that are included among the A's
can be deleted from the right hand side

As mentioned earlier, every FD implies an MVD

FD Promotion: Every FD is an MVD

If A1, A2, ..., An → B1, B2, ..., Bm then A1, A2, ..., An ↠ B1, B2, ..., Bm

To see this, consider two tuples, t and u that agree on the A's. The tuple u is a
tuple that agrees with t on the B's and with u on all other attributes.

MVD's, however, do *not* have a splitting rule

As an example: In the relation from 5.3.1, we have MVD
StudentID↠Program,Course,Section but StudentID↠Program,Course does NOT hold

If such an MVD *WERE* to be true, then, since the relation contains the tuples
(712318791,COMP,1001,101,Morningside,Paul) and
(712318791,COMP,1011,31,Stewart,Mary) the MVD would also require the tuple
(712318791,COMP,1001,31,Stewart,Mary) but there is no guarantee that a section 31 of
COMP1001 even exists, and if it does, student 712318791 would probably not be
registered in it, since he/she is registered in section 101 of COMP1001.

There are, however, properties of MVD's that are quite different from those of FD's

One such property is the *Complementation Rule*

If A1, A2, ..., An ↠ B1, B2, ..., Bm then A1, A2, ..., An ↠ C1, C2, ..., Cp where
C1,C2, ..., Cp is the collection of all attributes not among the A's or B's

Example: since StudentID↠ProgramCourseSection holds in our example, then
StudentID↠ParentLastName ParentFirstName must also hold

Design Theory for Relational Databases: Normal Forms

5.4 Fourth Normal Form

A relation R is said to be in *fourth* normal form (4NF) if for any nontrivial MVD, $A_1,\ldots,A_n \twoheadrightarrow B_1,\ldots,B_m$ the left side $\{A_1,\ldots,A_n\}$ must be a superkey.

– Notice the similarity between 4NF and BCNF

Since every FD is an MVD, every 4NF relation is a BCNF relation, so every BCNF violation is a 4NF violation. There are, however, BCNF relations that are not 4NF.

The relation in 5.3.1 is an example.

5.4.1 Decomposition into Fourth Normal Form

There is a 4NF decomposition algorithm which is very similar to the BCNF decomposition algorithm

INPUT: A relation R0 and a set S0 of MVD's

OUTPUT: A decomposition of R0 into relations, all of which are in 4NF, and which has the lossless join property

METHOD: Do the following, starting with R = R0 and S = S0

Find a 4NF violation in R

An MVD $A_1,\ldots,A_n \twoheadrightarrow B_1,\ldots,B_m$ with $\{A_1,\ldots,A_n\}$ not a superkey

If no such violation exists, return R

If there is such a violation, divide R into two relations

R1 with attributes $\{A_1,\ldots,A_n, B_1,\ldots,B_m\}$

R2 with attributes $\{A_1,\ldots,A_n, C_1,\ldots,C_p\}$ where $\{C_1,\ldots,C_p\}$ is the collection of attributes not in $\{A_1,\ldots,A_n, B_1,\ldots,B_m\}$

Identify the MVD's (and FD's) S1 and S2, that hold in R1 and R2 respectively

Repeat with R = R1 , S=S1 and R = R2, S=S2

5.4.2 Relationships Among Normal Forms

4NF implies BCNF and BCNF implies 3NF

Decomposition into BCNF removes redundancies due to FD's

A relation in BCNF will have no FD redundancies.

Decomposition into 4NF removes redundancies due to MVD's.

5.4.3 An Algorithm for Discovering MVD's

Reasoning about MVD's (or combinations of FD's and MVD's) tends to be much more difficult than reasoning about FD's alone, but the idea behind the "Chase" technique can be extended to apply to MVD's as well as FD's.

Design Theory for Relational Databases: Normal Forms

5.4.3.1 Closure and Chase with FD's

For FD's we have a "closure" algorithm to determine whether one FD follows from some given FD's. (In fact, this "closure" algorithm is essentially the same as the chase algorithm.)

We have seen how, given a set X of attributes, we can compute its closure X+ with respect to a set of FD's.

An FD X→Y follows from a set F of FD's if Y⊆X+, the closure of X with respect to F.

We can view the computation of the closure as a variant of the chase, using different starting tableau and different goal condition.

> We start with a tableau with two rows, with entries equal in attributes of X and different in all other attributes.

> We then apply the FD's in F to chase this tableau.

> The FD's will result in equal entries in columns of attributes in X+

5.4.3.1.1 Closure and Chase with FD's: Example

Consider a relation R(A,B,C,D,E,F) with FD's AB→C, BC→AD, D→E, and CF→B

We would like to determine whether AB→D

> We start with FDTableau#1
>
> > (Note that attributes A and B have the same values in both rows.)

A	B	C	D	E	F
a	b	c1	d1	e1	f1
a	b	c2	d2	e2	f2
			FDTableau#1		

> We apply AB→C to conclude that the C entries must be equal.
>
> > (This gives us FDTableau#2)

A	B	C	D	E	F
a	b	c1	d1	e1	f1
a	b	c1	d2	e2	f2
			FDTableau#2		

> We next apply BC→AD to infer d1=d2 and apply D→E to infer e1=e2
>
> > Which brings us to FDTableau#3.

A	B	C	D	E	F
a	b	c1	d1	e1	f1
a	b	c1	d1	e1	f2
			FDTableau#3		

Since the entries in the D column agree, we can conclude that AB→D does, in fact, follow from the given FD's.

5.4.3.2 Extending the Chase to MVD's

The major difference between FD's and MVD's, from the point of view of the chase, is that, while an FD tends to show us that (existing) entries in a given column, must be equal, an MVD will imply that there must be another tuple in the relation, having attribute values equal to those of existing tuples.

Design Theory for Relational Databases: Normal Forms

5.4.3.2.1 Extending the Chase to MVD's: Example 1

Suppose we have a relation R(A,B,C,D) with dependencies A→B and B↠C and we want to determine whether A↠C

We begin with a tableau MVDTableau#1. Since we are interested in analyzing A↠C, our tableau must have two tuples that agree on attribute A. What we need to show is that there must be a tuple (a.b,c,d) in the tableau if both A→B and B↠C hold.

A	B	C	D
a	b1	c	d1
a	b	c2	d

MVDTableau#1

First we apply the FD A→B. Both tuples have the same entry in attribute A, and so must also have the same value in attribute B. This gives us MVDTableau#2.

A	B	C	D
a	b	c	d1
a	b	c2	d

MVDTableau#2

Now if MVD B↠C is to hold, and if t1=(a,b,c,d1) and t2=(a,b,c2,d) are tuples in R, then v1=(a,b,c,d) and v2=(a,b,c2.d1) must also be tuples in R.

(As MVDTableau#3.)

A	B	C	D
a	b	c	d1
a	b	c2	d
a	b	c	d
a	b	c2	d1

MVDTableau#3

Since the tuple (a,b,c,d) must be in R, we can conclude that A↠C holds in R.

5.4.3.2.2 Extending the Chase to MVD's: Example 2

There is another (possibly somewhat surprising rule) for combining MVD's and FD's

If X↠Y, if Z⊆Y and if there is any W→Z then X→Z

We will use the chase to verify a (relatively simple) example of the application of this rule:

Suppose R(A,B,C,D) is a relation in which dependencies A↠BC and D→C hold. Then this rule would imply that A→C also holds in R

We begin with RuleTableau#1:

We must establish that, given these dependencies, c1 must be equal to c2.

A	B	C	D
a	b1	c1	d1
a	b2	c2	d2

RuleTableau#1

Since we have tuples (which we can designate as t1 and t2) with equal values in attribute A, the MVD A→→BC implies that there must also exist tuples u1 and u2 whose values in column A are also equal to that of t1 and t2, and are such that:

The B and C values of u1 are equal to those of t1 and all other values (attribute D) are equal to those of t2

The B and C values of u2 are equal to those of t2 and all other values (attribute D) are equal to those of t1

(See RuleTableau#2)

A	B	C	D
a	b1	c1	d1
a	b2	c2	d2
a	b1	c1	d2
a	b2	c2	d1

RuleTableau#2

In t1 we have attribute D equal to d1 and attribute C equal to c1 and in tuple u2 attribute D is also d1 while attribute C is c2, so the FD D→C implies that c2 = c1

(RuleTableau#3)

A	B	C	D
a	b1	c1	d1
a	b2	c1	d2
a	b1	c1	d2
a	b2	c1	d1

RuleTableau#3

This, then, establishes that the FD A→C must hold in relation R.

5.5 Why the Chase Works, FD's and MVD's

When applying the "Chase", at each step in the process we are either identifying equal values of attributes or creating new tuples. Each step is an observation of a fact that must be true about the relation due to properties (FD's or MVD's) that must hold for the relation.

Therefore, any result that we can conclude must be true for the relation.

If, on the other hand, we reach a point where no more changes can be made, and the desired result cannot be concluded, the resulting tableau will be an example of a relation in which all dependencies hold and in which the desired result is not true.

Design Theory for Relational Databases: Normal Forms

5.6 Chapter 5 Questions

5.6.1 True-False

5.6.1.1 The goal of decomposition is to replace a single relation with several that have no anomalies.

5.6.1.2 No relation with only two attributes can be in BCNF.

5.6.1.3 If a relation is decomposed according to the algorithm described in Section 5.1.3.1 of this text, all of the information can be recovered faithfully by the natural join.

5.6.1.4 A "multivalued dependency" is an assertion that two attributes, or sets of attributes, are independent of one another.

5.6.1.5 If $\{B_1,...,B_m\}$ is contained in $\{A_1,...,A_n\}$ then $A_1,...,A_n \twoheadrightarrow B_1,...,B_m$.

5.6.1.6 If $A_1, A_2, ..., A_n \twoheadrightarrow B_1, B_2, ..., B_m$ then $A_1, A_2, ..., A_n \rightarrow B_1, B_2, ..., B_m$.

5.6.1.7 BCNF implies 4NF.

5.6.1.8 The idea behind the chase algorithm can be extended to apply to MVD's as well as FD's.

5.6.1.9 The major difference between FD's and MVD's, from the point of view of the chase, is that, while an MVD tends to show us that (existing) entries in a given column, must be equal, an FD will imply that there must be another tuple in the relation, having component values those of existing tuples, but swapped.

5.6.2 Multiple Choice

5.6.2.1 If it is possible to obtain all of the information in a relation from a decomposition, then the decomposition is called a _____
   a. lossless join
   b. faithful join
   c. lossless projection
   d. faithful projection
   e. none of the above

5.6.2.2 The natural join is:
   a. both associative and commutative
   b. associative but not commutative
   c. commutative but not associative
   d. neither associative nor commutative
   e. none of the above

5.6.3 Completion

5.6.3.1 A relation R is in _____ if, the left side of every nontrivial FD contains a key.

5.6.3.2 We begin the chase test by drawing a "picture" (called a _____) illustrating what we know, putting subscripts on unknown values (subscripts identifying the projection.)

5.6.3.3 An attribute that is a member of some key is sometimes said to be _____.

Chapter 6 High Level Database Models – E/R Diagrams

The creation of a database will typically involve a number of phases, and is generally carried out most effectively if approached in a "top-down" manner (as is common in computer applications,)

The desired end result would (almost certainly) be implemented using a *relational DBMS*.

Before creating the DBMS code, one will normally describe the intended system as a collection of *database schema*.

Before specifying/writing the schema for the system one must identify exactly what information must be represented and what kinds of interrelationships among the various kinds of information must be represented. (This phase of the process is referred to as the *High Level Design* phase.)

Before getting involved in the design of a system, one must, of course, have a reasonably clear understanding of what it is that is to be represented in the database.

Although almost all commercial database managers use the relational model, it is usually easier to start with a higher level model and then convert to schemas related to the relational model.

The relational model is limited, it has only *one* concept, the *relation*.

Simplicity of concepts is an advantage when it comes to efficient implementation of design concepts, but can be a weakness in preliminary design.

In preliminary design, it is often helpful to begin description using a higher level design model.

6.1 High Level Design

In the High-Level Design phase of database development, we deal with questions like:

What information will be stored?

How information elements are related to each other?

What constraints will be involved in the system?
    We must consider constraints on the data
    And also constraints on interrelationships.

This high level design phase may last a long time, and might well be revisited several times during the process of creating the database.

6.1.1 Notations for High Level Design Development

There are several options for the notation in which the design might be expressed.

The oldest method is the "entity-relationship diagram".

A more recent trend is the use of UML (Unified Modelling Language.)

UML was originally designed for describing object-oriented software projects but has been adapted to describe database schemas as well.

Another method is the use of ODL (Object Description Language) which was created to describe databases as collections of classes and their objects.

Commercial DBMS systems are almost all relational, so after the design phase is complete, the high level design must be converted to a relational design.

The advantage of using one of these standard notations for high level development is that there is a fairly mechanical way of converting the design into a relational database schema which will run on a conventional DBMS.

High Level Database Models – E/R Diagrams

6.2 The Entity/Relationship Model

In the entity-relationship model (E/R model) the structure of data is represented graphically as an E/R diagram using three principal element types:

Entity sets

Attributes

Relationships

6.2.1 Entity Sets

In an E/R diagram, an *entity* represents an object of some sort, and an *entity set* is a collection of similar entities

Examples: In our college database:

Each student is an entity and the collection of all students is an entity set.

Faculty members are entities and the collection of all faculty members is an entity set.

Classes are entities and the collection of all classes is an entity set.

6.2.2 Attributes

Entity sets have associated *attributes*, by which we mean *properties* of the entities in the set

Examples:

Entities in the entity set "Personnel" have attributes "IDNumber", "SocSecNum", "LastName", "FirstName" and "Gender".

Among the attributes for entities in the entity set "Classes" are "ProgramID", "CourseNumber", "SectionNumber", "RoomID" and "TeacherIDNumber".

It is common for entity sets to be implemented as *relations*.

There do exist E/R model systems in which attributes can be structured types, but we will assume that all attribute values are of primitive data types.

6.2.3 Relationships

Relationships are connections between entity sets.

Examples:

"Classes", "Faculty" and "Students" are three entity sets.

There is an obvious relationship "Teaches/TaughtBy" between "Classes" and "Faculty".

A relationship "EnrolledIn" connects "Classes" and "Students".

6.2.4 Entity-Relationship Diagrams

An ER diagram is a graph representing entity sets, attributes and relationships.

Elements of these types are represented by nodes of the graph and are distinguished by using different shapes for different kinds of entities:[9]

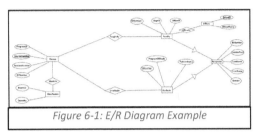

Entity sets are represented as rectangles

Attributes are represented by ovals

Relationships are represented by diamonds

Edges/lines connect entity sets with their attributes and relationships with their entity sets.

Figure 6-1: E/R Diagram Example

It is common for there to be restrictions on "*multiplicities*" of a relationship.

6.2.4.1 Entity-Relationship Diagrams: "Many-Many" Relationships

In general, a binary relationship can connect multiple entities in one entity set with multiple entries in the other. This kind of relationship is called a "*many-many*" relationship.

Example: The "EnrolledIn" relationship in Figure 6-1 is a many-many relationship. A student will typically be enrolled in more than one class and a class will normally have more than one student enrolled in it.

6.2.4.2 Entity-Relationship Diagrams: "Many-One" Relationships

Suppose R is a relationship between entity sets E and F. If each member of E can be connected by R to *at most one* member of F, we say that R is a

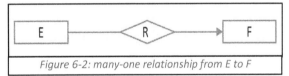

Figure 6-2: many-one relationship from E to F

many-one relationship from E to F (or *one-many* from F to E.) In E/R diagrams, we use arrows to designate multiplicities of relationships. A many-one relationship from E to F would de identified using an arrow pointing to F. (See Figure 6-2)

The arrow pointing to F indicates that that a member of E is related to at most one member of F. If the idea is to require that each member of E is related to *exactly* one member of F, then we would use a rounded arrow, rather than a pointed arrow (as in Figure 6-3.)

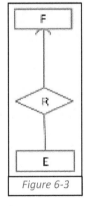

Figure 6-3

---

[9]   There are a number of different E/R notations available. The notations described here are adapted from those in *"A First Course in Database Systems"* by Ullman and Widom.

Example: Faculty members are normally assigned offices to use while preparing classes, to meet students, etc.

The relation "OfficeOf" is (probably) many-one from "Faculty" to "Offices", since a teacher will be assigned only one office, but offices might well be assigned to multiple faculty members. It is also possible that a faculty member might not have an office assigned (adjunct faculty, newly hired faculty, …)

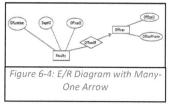

Figure 6-4: E/R Diagram with Many-One Arrow

6.2.4.3 One-One Relationships

If R is both one-many from E to F and many-one from E to F, we say that R is *one-one*. A one-one relationship between E and F would have arrows pointing to both E and F.

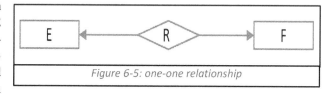

Figure 6-5: one-one relationship

Students and faculty have many characteristics in common (names, id numbers, social security numbers, genders.) There are advantages in using a common entity set for these values. With such a "Personnel" entity set, each faculty member (identified by "IDNumber") would be associated with a unique "Personnel" entry and each student (also identified by "IDNumber") would also be associated with a unique "Personnel" entry. The two relationships "FacultyIDMatch" and "StudentIDMatch" in Figure 6-6 require that each faculty member and each student is related to exactly one "Personnel" entity but a "Personnel" entry is related to at most one student and/or at most one faculty member.

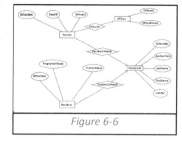

Figure 6-6

6.2.4.4 Entity-Relationship Diagrams: Attributes on Relationships

Sometimes it is desirable to associate an attribute with a *relationship* rather than an entity. In an E/R diagram we depict such a relation attribute in the same way that we do with attributes on entity sets, with an oval and a line connecting the oval to the relationship diamond.

Example: In any college there will be a relationship between students and classes, identifying which classes each student is enrolled in. Colleges also often provide different *types* of enrollment (pass-fail, auditing, …) These types might naturally be identified as attributes of the enrollment relation. (See Figure 6-7.)

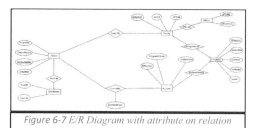

Figure 6-7 E/R Diagram with attribute on relation

6.2.4.5 Entity-Relationship Diagrams: Higher Order Relationships

The E/R model makes it easy to define relationships involving more than two entity sets.

In practice, ternary and higher order relations tend to be rare, but they can be useful occasionally when it is necessary to describe certain kinds of situations.

In an E/R diagram, such a *multiway relation* can be depicted as a relation diamond with lines to each of the entity sets involved.

6.2.4.6 Entity-Relationship Diagrams: Entity Set for Attribute Values

When a desired relationship attribute is complex, it can be better to create an entity set for its possible values, and use a multiway relationship referencing values in that entity set.

This kind of structure can save storage space if (as in the case of enrollment types) there are a limited number of attribute values. It is especially valuable if these attribute values are relatively large.

(This is not the case in this particular example.)

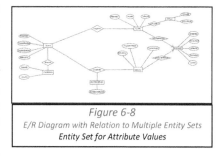

Figure 6-8
E/R Diagram with Relation to Multiple Entity Sets
Entity Set for Attribute Values

Limiting attribute values to the values in an entity set also eliminates typographical errors, since it limits the possible values in the relation to those in that entity set.

6.2.4.7 Entity-Relationship Diagrams: Converting Multiway Relations to Binary

Although some data models only represent *binary* relationships[10], multiway relationships are often useful in construction of some kinds of databases and the E/R model does support them.

Since different data models have different strengths and weaknesses, it is often useful to convert a description from one system to another.

In the process of converting from a description using E/R diagrams to another data model, the multiway relations usually require special treatment. A multiway relationship can be converted to a binary relationship using the following process:

First introduce a new entity set whose entities are tuples of the relationship set for the multiway relation.

(We call this set a *connecting entity set*.)

We then introduce many-one relationships from the connecting entity set to each of the entity sets that provide components of tuples in the original multiway relationship.

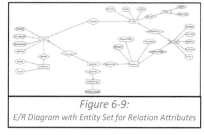

Figure 6-9:
E/R Diagram with Entity Set for Relation Attributes

Note that in our example diagram, the connecting entity set "EnrolledIn" will have as (primary key) all of the attributes that appear as primary keys for "Classes", "Student" and "EnrollmentType". It is inconvenient to display all of these attributes in this illustration (and, as we will see shortly, it is also unnecessary to do so.)

---

10 UML and ODL are among them.

6.2.4.8 Entity-Relationship Diagrams: Subclasses

Often an entity set includes certain members that have special properties not associated with all members of the set.

If so, we might define special-case entity sets (subclasses) in which the tuples have their own special attributes and/or relationships.

We connect such a subclass to its parent class with a special kind of relationship called an *isa*.

(A *is a* B)

In an E/R diagram, an *isa* relationship is identified using a triangle, rather than a diamond.

We do not need to draw arrows in an isa diagram since *every* isa relationship is inherently one-one.

Examples: Both "Faculty" and "Students" are types of "Personnel"

A student "*is a*" *person*.

A special kind of a "*person*" having special kinds of attributes not shared by all kinds of personnel.

A faculty member "*is a*" *person*.

A special kind of a "*person*" having special kinds of attributes not shared by all kinds of personnel.

It is natural to identify these relationships as isa relationships.

We can easily recognize that there are a number of different classes of students, some of which require specialized treatment.

Some students have athletic scholarships.

Some students have physical handicaps that require that they receive special accommodation.

Some students are noncitizens.

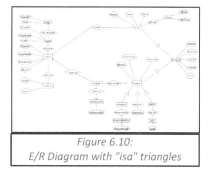

Figure 6.10:
E/R Diagram with "isa" triangles

Observe that a noncitizen would have only one country of origin, but a handicapped student might require multiple types of accommodations and that an athlete might participate in more than one sport.

6.3 Design Principles

Although there are many more details about the E/R model that might be covered, we should first discuss what constitutes a "*good*" design (and what kinds of things should be avoided.)

6.3.1 Good Design requires "Faithfulness"

First and foremost, the design should be *faithful* to the specifications of the application.

Entity sets and their attributes should reflect reality, as should relations between the entity sets.

Attribute "Gender" makes sense for an entity set "Personnel" but not for an entity set "Classes".

An attribute "Horsepower" might be reasonable for a class named "Automobiles" but would just be silly for "Faculty".

It is not always obvious exactly *what* the real world requirements of a situation are.

Consider the relation "TaughtBy" connecting entity sets "Classes" and "Faculty".

Should this relation be many-many or many-one?

If the institution supports *team teaching*, the relationship would be many-many. If each class has a unique teacher, the relationship would be many-one. You need to know the institutional policies in order to design a college database.

One must have a good understanding of the reality that a database is to represent before beginning the design process.

One should also recognize that this "reality" is likely to change over time.

6.3.2 Good Design avoids Redundancy

We have already mentioned some of the problems that redundancy can cause, and in the E/R model, there are several mechanisms which can introduce redundancy (as well as other kinds of anomalies.)

Example: The college administration might suggest that the "Students" entity set should include an attribute for the number of credits in which the student is enrolled.

Such an attribute would simplify certain kinds of computations (and, as a result, many common queries would execute faster) but such an attribute would create the potential for update anomalies[11].

A student might withdraw from a class or add a new class. In either case, the potential exists for the system to fail to update the attribute in such a "NumberOfCredits" attribute.

Simplicity counts. One should generally avoid introducing more elements than necessary into a design.

---

[11] It would also increase storage space requirements.

6.3.3 Good Design involves "Choosing the Right Relationships"

Entity sets can generally be connected by various relationships, but including every possible relationship is usually not a good idea. Doing that can lead to redundancy, update anomalies and deletion anomalies. (Recall the problem that would arise upon adding a "NumberOfCredits" attribute to the "Students" entity set. The value that would be stored could also be computed as the sum of the credits in classes in which a student was enrolled.)

6.3.3.1 Picking the Right Kind of Element

We often have options regarding the kind of design element to use to represent a real world concept. We must often choose between representing something as an attribute or as a relationship with an entity set.

Attributes tend to be easier to implement than entity sets and/or relationships, but too many attributes make entities complex and difficult to manipulate.

Too many attributes can cause other kinds of problems as well.

6.4 Constraints in the E/R Model

The E/R model provides several ways to describe common constraints on the data that would populate a database that is being designed.

Among the kinds of constraints that the E/R model can express are that of:

of being a key for an entity set,

of having referential integrity,

of having constrained connectivity degrees.

6.4.1 Key for an Entity Set

The E/R diagram system provides a technique for specifying that an attribute, or a collection of attributes, is a (primary) key for an entity set. We indicate the key for an entity set by underlining the attribute name(s).

Recall that a *key* for an entity set E is a set K of one or more attributes such that two distinct entities in E cannot have identical values for the attributes in K. If the set K includes more than one attribute, it is permitted for two entries in E to have the same value for one attribute, or more than one attribute, but they cannot have the same values for all the attributes in K.

There are some important points concerning keys, that should be remembered:

Every entity set should have a key.

In some cases the key, or part of the key, actually belongs to another entity set (*isa* hierarchies and "*weak*" entity sets.)

There can be more than one key for an entity set, but it is customary to pick one key as the "primary key" and act as if that were the only key.

When an entity set is involved in an isa-hierarchy, we require that the root entity set have all the attributes needed for a key and that the key for each entity is found from its component in the root entity set, regardless of how many entity sets in the hierarchy have components for the entity.

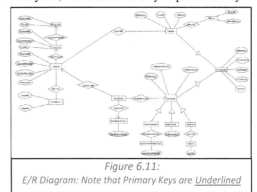

Figure 6.11:
E/R Diagram: Note that Primary Keys are <u>Underlined</u>

6.4.2 Referential Integrity

A *referential-integrity* constraint requires that a value appearing in one context must also appear in another

Example: Consider the arrow at the "Faculty" end of the relationship, "TaughtBy", from "Classes" to "Faculty. Relationships specified using *simple* arrows (arrows with sharp points), as in this case, indicate a "many-one" relationship but these arrows do not specify referential integrity constraints. The *simple* arrow indicates that a "Class" will be taught by *no more than* one "Faculty" member but might not be assigned to be taught by anybody.

We can use a *rounded* arrow, rather than a pointed arrow, in an E/R diagram to indicate that each entity must relate to *exactly* one entity rather than *no more than* one entity.

A *rounded* arrow pointing from an entity set E to another entity set F indicates that each entity in E is related to *exactly* one element in F.

In the E/R diagram in Figure 6-11, the rounded head on the "Classes" end of the "ClassEnroll" relation indicates that each "EnrolledIn" entity is related to exactly one "Classes" entity. The rounded arrow at the "Students" end of the "StudentEnroll" relation indicates that each "EnrolledIn" entity is related to exactly one "Students" entity. The rounded arrow at the "EnrollmentType" end of the "TypeEnroll" relation indicates that each "EnrolledIn" entity is related to exactly one "EnrollmentType" entity.

In the Figure 6-11 diagram sharp arrows are used to indicate that:

a class will be taught by at most one faculty member (possibly nobody is assigned yet?)

a faculty member is assigned at most one office (but might not have been assigned an office.)

6.4.3 Degree Constraints

In an E/R diagram, we can attach *bounding numbers* to the edges that attach relations to entity sets. These bounding numbers establish limits on the number of entities that can be connected.

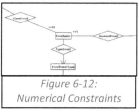

Figure 6-12:
Numerical Constraints

In the example at the right, Figure 6-12, classes are limited to no more than 35 student enrollments and each student it limited to no more than 5 enrollments.

(A pointed arrow would be equivalent to constraint "<=1". A rounded arrow is equivalent to constraint "=1".)

6.5 Weak Entity Sets in the E/R Model

Recall that each entity set *should* have a *key*. It is possible (in fact quite common) for the key of an entity set to be composed of attributes, some or all of which refer to the same things as those of another entity set. (examples: attributes "IDNumber" in "Classes" and "Faculty" and "Personnel" and in "Students" and "EnrolledIn". Attributes "OfficeID" in "Faculty" and "Offices".)

Under some conditions, such an entity set and the relation which the association determines, will form what we call a *weak entity set* and *weak relation* (we also call these *supporting* relations.)

In an E/R diagram, we use double borders to identify weak entity sets and weak relations.

6.5.1 Requirements for Weak Entity Sets

For a combination of an entity set and a relation to qualify as being a weak entity set and weak relation, they must satisfy certain conditions.

Not every entity set is a weak entity set and not every relation is a weak relation.

A relation R from an entity set E to another entity set F, the relation R qualifies as being *weak*, provided that:

The key for E consists of one or more key attributes that are part of a many-one relationship. (These many-one relationships are called *supporting relationships* and the entity sets reached by these relationships are *supporting entity sets*.)

The following conditions hold:
a) R is a binary, many-one relationship from E to F
b) R has referential integrity from E to F (For every E-entity, there must be exactly one existing F-entity related to it by R.)
c) The attributes that F supplies for the key in E must be the key attributes of F
d) If F itself is also weak, then some or all of the key attributes of F supplied to E will be key attributes of one or more entity sets G to which F is connected by a supporting relationship. Recursively, if G is weak, some key attributes of G will be supplied from elsewhere.
e) If there are several different supporting relationships from E to the same entity set F, then each relationship is used to supply a copy of the key attributes of F to help form the key of E. (An entity e of E may be related to different entities of F through different supporting relationships from E.)

Note that any "isa" relationship inherently satisfies the conditions for being a supporting relationship, and, thus is inherently a weak relationship.

6.5.2 Reasons for Weak Entity Sets

There are two principal reasons we might want to identify weak entity sets and relations:

Sometimes entity sets fall into a hierarchy, but not a hierarchy based on classifications related to an "isa hierarchy". If entities of set E are subunits of entities in set F it is possible that names of E entities are not unique until we take into account the name of the F unit to which E is subordinate.

In addition to isa related hierarchies, there is another common source of weak entity sets. They also occur due to the elimination of multiway relationships. The connecting entity sets created in this elimination process will, of necessity, be weak entity sets.

6.5.3 Examples of Weak Entity Sets

In addition to the "isa" relations, our ongoing "College" example includes three weak relations: "ClassEnroll", StudentEnroll" and "TypeEnroll", all related to the same weak entity set, "EnrolledIn" as well as weak relations "ClassCourse" and "CourseProgram".

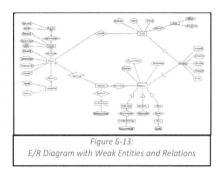

Figure 6-13:
E/R Diagram with Weak Entities and Relations

6.6 From E/R Diagrams to Relational Designs

As a general rule, the conversion of an E/R diagram into a relational database is straightforward:

For each entity set, create a relation with the same set of attributes.

For each relationship, create a relation whose attributes are the keys for the connected entity sets.

These two processes will deal with the great majority of the conversion, but there are several special situations that need to be dealt with somewhat differently:

Many-one relations can generally be represented simply as attributes in the "many" entity set.

This will usually be, not only simpler, but also result in more efficient computations, than would the creation of a separate relation to specify the relationship.

Weak-entity sets cannot (always) be translated in this straightforward way.

"isa" relationships and subclasses require especially careful treatment

Sometimes we need to combine relationships.

High Level Database Models – E/R Diagrams

6.6.1 Example: From Entity Sets to Relations

We will work with the example of the ER diagram in Figure 6-13.

6.6.1.1 Start with Normal (nonweak) Entity Sets

Recall that the "isa" entities are *inherently* weak.

In the diagram of Figure 6-13, the nonweak entity sets are: "AccommodationType", "Classroom", "Program", "EnrollmentType", "Offices", "Personnel", and "Sport"

For each, we create a relation of the same name with the same set of attributes:

AccommodationType (AccommodationID)

Classroom(RoomID, Capacity)

Program(ProgramID, DeptID)

EnrollmentType(EnrollTypeID)

Offices(OfficeID, OfficePhone)

Personnel(IDNumber, LastName, FirstName, Gender, SocSecNumber)

Sport(SportID)

6.6.1.2 NonWeak Relations

Our next step would be to define relations implementing *relationships*.

We would start with those connecting only nonweak entity sets. We would create relations with attributes including all (primary) key attributes of all connected entity sets, plus, of course, any attributes related to the relationship.

In Figure 6-14, we have added an entity set for "Department"

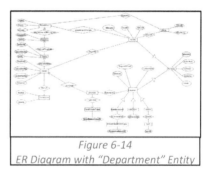

Figure 6-14
ER Diagram with "Department" Entity

Department(DeptID, OfficeID, ChairID)

with relations "DeptOffices", "DepartmentOfPrograms", and "DepartmentOfFaculty". The first two of these do not involve any weak entity sets.

In the example of Figure 6-14 the only relationships connecting just nonweak entity sets are "DeptOffices" and "DepartmentOfPrograms"

Relations implementing these relationships would be:

DeptOffices(DeptID, OfficeID)

DepartmentOfPrograms(DeptID, ProgramID)

6.6.1.2.1 Combining Relations

Sometimes, as in this case, the relations we get as described above are not the best possible choice for representing relationships. A common situation occurs when there is an entity set E with a many-one relation R to an entity set F. As described earlier, instead of creating a new relation for R we can represent the relation R by simply adding attribute(s) to the representation for E with values the primary key for F, as well as any attributes of R. Because R is many-one, the key attributes of E functionally determine any attributes of R as well as the key attributes of F. Hence, we can combine all into one relation:

1. All attributes of E

2. Key attributes of F

3. Any attributes of R

For any entity e of E not related to an entity of F, the entries of type 2 and 3 would be null. Combining relations in this manner can result in more efficient data storage and faster search times.

Of course, if R is not many-one, such a combination could lead to redundancy, since representing connections to multiple entries in F would require more than one entry in E with the same "primary key" values.

In the example of Figure 6-14, both "DeptOffices" and "DepartmentOfPrograms" are many-one relationships and so, instead of representing them as separate relations, we could represent them as attributes for primary keys of "Department" and "Offices" in the "Program" and "Department" relations:

Program(ProgramID, **DeptID**)

Department(DeptID, **OfficeID**)

6.6.1.3 Weak Entity Sets and Weak Relations

A weak entity set needs to be handled differently than a normal (nonweak) entity set. (We distinguish between weak entity relations and isa relations. "isa" relations are dealt with somewhat differently and will be covered later.)

The relation for a weak entity set W must include not only the attributes of W, but also the key attributes from the supporting entity sets.

In an E/R diagram a supporting entity is identified with double line boundaries. They are reached through weak *relationships* (double diamonds in an E/R diagram.)

The relation for any relationship in which the weak entity set appears must use all its key attributes, including those that appear in other entity sets. A supporting relationship from a weak entity set to a supporting entity set need not be converted to a relation. It is (by definition) a many-one relationship and is dealt by including the primary key(s) in the representation of the entity set, just as is done for any other many one relationship.

In dealing with weak entity sets we must:

Identify any weak entity set(s) whose weak relation will have primary keys from supporting entity sets for which relations have already been created (which would imply that their key attributes have been identified and defined.)

In the example of Figure 6-14, weak entity set "Courses" and weak relation "CourseProgram" is such a situation. "Program" is a supporting entity set for "Courses" and its key attribute, "ProgramID", has been identified. This allows us to implement "CourseProgram" by means of an attribute, "ProgramID", in entity set "Courses".

Courses(<u>ProgramID</u>, <u>CourseNumber</u>, Credits)

We could now treat this entity set as if it were a normal (nonweak) entity set. Create relations corresponding to any (nonsupporting) relationships between this entity set and other established relations (there are none in Figure 6-14) We will also be able to use it as a supporting relation for other weak relationships.

After identifying the key for "Courses" we can begin the process of implementing the weak relationship "ClassCourse" as attributes with values from attributes "ProgramID" and "CourseNumber" of entity set "Course".

Classes(<u>ProgramID</u>, <u>CourseNumber</u>, <u>SectionNumber</u>,)

The relation "Classes", however, also has a (weak) many-one relationship "TaughtBy" to the weak entity set "Faculty"

"Faculty" is also a weak entity set because it has an "isa" relationship with "Personnel".

6.6.1.4 "isa" Relations

When some entities in a system have special properties not associated with other similar entities it can be convenient to divide the set into *subclasses*.

In our example, students and faculty are two different kinds of people (i.e. personnel.) They have some common attributes (Social security numbers, genders, …) but each subclass has some attributes that the other does not.

Faculty have offices (at least some do) but students do not. A "Student" has a "tuitionstatus" but a faculty member does not.

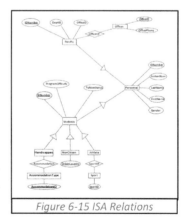

Figure 6-15 ISA Relations

In an E/R diagram, we identify such subclass relationships using triangle in place of diamond shapes.

When we have an isa-hierarchy of entity sets, there will be a *root* entity, and this entity will have a key that identifies each entity represented by the structure.

92

High Level Database Models – E/R Diagrams

When we are constructing relations, there are several strategies that might be used for representing an "isa" hierarchy:

1. *Follow the E/R viewpoint*: For each entity E in the hierarchy, create a relation that includes the key attributes from the root and any unique attributes belonging to E

2. *Treat entities as objects belonging to a single class*: For each possible subtree (that includes the root, which constitutes a subtree with only one node) create a relation whose schema include all attributes of entity sets in the subtree.

3. *Use null values*: Create one relation with all attributes of all entity sets in the hierarchy. Each entity is represented by a tuple. A tuple will have null values for any attribute that the entity represented by that tuple does not have.

6.6.1.4.1 "isa" Relations: E/R Viewpoint

With this approach, we create a relation for each entity set.

If an entity set E is not the root of the hierarchy, then the relation for E will contain the key from the root (to identify each tuple), as well as all attributes unique to E

If E is involved in a relationship, the key attribute(s) (from the root) identify the entities of E in the relation corresponding to that relationship.

Note that, although we describe "isa" as being a "relationship", isa relationships are different from other types of relationships.

An isa relationship connects tuples representing the same entity, rather than different entities.

We do NOT create a separate relation to represent an isa "relationship".

"isa" relationships are inherently one-one relationships.

In our example, using this approach, we would create relations:

Personnel(<u>IDNumber</u>, SocSecNum, LastName, FirstName, Gender)

Faculty(<u>IDNumber</u>, OfficeID, DeptID)

Students(<u>IDNumber</u>, ProgramOfStudy, TuitionStatus)

The "Faculty" entity set is involved in relationships"OfficeOf", "TaughtBy" and "DepartmentOfFaculty". The relations "OfficeOf" and "DepartmentOfFaculty" are implemented by the "OfficeID""DeptID" attribute in "Faculty". The relation "TaughtBy" would be implemented by adding the primary key as an attribute in "Classes"

Classes(<u>ProgramID</u>, <u>CourseNumber</u>, <u>SectionNumber</u>, IDNumber)

The "Students" entity set is the supporting entity set for three more isa relations, and, once we have identified its (root) attributes, we can implement the relationships that involve it.

Handicapped(<u>IDNumber</u>)
NonCitizen(<u>IDNumber</u>, OriginCountry)
Athlete(<u>IDNumber</u>)

93

The "Handicapped" and "Athlete" entity sets are also involved in relationships "Accommodation" and "SportOf". Now that we have the identified the primary keys for the entity sets, we can implement the relationships.

Accommodation(<u>IDNumber</u>, <u>AccommodationID</u>)

SportOf(<u>IDNumber</u>, <u>SportID</u>)

Now we have identified primary keys for "Students", "Classes" and "EnrollmentType".

These are all of the relationships involving entity set "EnrolledIn" and all of them are many one relations and are implemented as attributes with corresponding primary key values.

EnrolledIn(<u>ProgramID</u>, <u>CourseNumber</u>, <u>SectionNumber</u>, <u>IDNumber</u>, <u>EnrollmentTypeID</u>)

Each student will be represented in the "Students" relation, and, possibly, in one or more of the other relations ("Handicapped", "Noncitizen", "Athlete") as well. Thus, many students will have multiple records.

This, then, illustrates one way that the ER Viewpoint approach can introduce redundancy and permit update anomalies.

6.6.1.4.2 "isa" Relations: Objects belonging to a Single Class

An alternative strategy for converting "isa" hierarchies into relations is to enumerate all possible subtrees of the hierarchy, and then create a relation for each subtree. A schema for a subtree would include all attributes of any entity set in the subtree.

In our example, the collection of subtrees in our student "isa" hierarchy would be:

TS = {"Students"}
   TS(<u>IDNumber</u>, ProgramOfStudy, TuitionStatus)
TSH = {"Student", "Handicap"}
   TSH(<u>IDNumber</u>, ProgramOfStudy, TuitionStatus,)
   TSHAccommodationRef(<u>IDNumber</u>, <u>AccommodationID</u>)
TSN={"Student", "NonCitizens"}
   TSN(<u>IDNumber</u>, ProgramOfStudy, TuitionStatus, OriginCountry)
TSA={"Student","Athlete"}
   TSA(<u>IDNumber</u>, ProgramOfStudy, TuitionStatus)
   TSASportOfAthlete(<u>IDNumber</u>, <u>SportID</u>)
TSHN={"Student","Handicap","NonCitizens"}
   TSHN(<u>IDNumber</u>, ProgramOfStudy, TuitionStatus, OriginCountry)
   TSHNAccommodationRef(<u>IDNumber</u>, <u>AccommodationID</u>)
TSHA={"Student", "Handicap", "Athlete"}
   TSHA(<u>IDNumber</u>, ProgramOfStudy, TuitionStatus)
   TSHAAccommodationRef(<u>IDNumber</u>, <u>AccommodationID</u>)
   TSHASportOfAthlete(<u>IDNumber</u>, <u>SportID</u>)
TSNA={"Student","NonCitizens","Athlete"}
   TSNA(<u>IDNumber</u>, ProgramOfStudy, TuitionStatus, OriginCountry)
   TSNASportOfAthlete(<u>IDNumber</u>, <u>SportID</u>)
TSHNA={"Student","Handicap",NonCitizens","Athlete"}
   TSHNA(<u>IDNumber</u>, ProgramOfStudy, TuitionStatus, OriginCountry)
   TSHNASportOfAthlete(<u>IDNumber</u>, <u>SportID</u>)
   TSHNAAccommodationRef(<u>IDNumber</u>, <u>AccommodationID</u>)

With this system, we have the option of representing each student with only have one record in one relation and use only the attributes appropriate for that type of student. This provides the most efficient option in terms of storage space and eliminates redundancy and update anomalies. Queries will be less efficient, however, since it might be necessary to search multiple records to find a student.

We might also record each student in every appropriate relation. This would optimize search time in certain types of queries (for example, to find all handicapped noncitizens, one need only search TSHN, rather than both TSHN and TSHNA.) With this system, however, there will be redundancy (some students would appear in multiple relations) but this can be offset somewhat by the elimination of multiple appearances of attributes.

6.6.1.4.3 "isa" Relations: Null Values

If we permit the use of the NULL value as a value in our tuples, then we can handle a hierarchy of entity sets with a single relation. In this system, the schema for the "isa" hierarchy in our ongoing College example would be:

Students(<u>IDNumber</u>, ProgramOfStudy, TuitionStatus, OriginCountry)

The tuple representing any student who is a citizen might have NULL in the "OriginCountry".

6.6.1.4.4 Comparison of Approaches for "isa" Relations

Each of the three approaches has its advantages and disadvantages, and there are several issues to be considered in choosing among them

1. It can be expensive to answer queries involving several relations, so we would prefer to find all attributes needed for a query in the same relation

2. We would not like to use too many relations

3. We would like to avoid repeating information, and minimize storage space

6.6.1.4.4.1 Comparison of Approaches for "isa" Relations – Issue #1

It can be expensive to answer queries involving several relations, so we would prefer to find all attributes needed for a query in one relation

The nulls approach uses only one relation with all possible attributes, so it has an advantage in this regard.

The other two approaches have advantages for different kinds of queries. For some kinds of queries the subtree approach is better and there are queries for which the E/R approach is advantageous.

6.6.1.4.4.2 Comparison of Approaches for "isa" Relations – Issue #2

We would not like to use too many relations. Numerous relations create a complex structure and can make future programming difficult and error prone.

Clearly the nulls approach is best in this area, since it involves only one relation. The straight E/R approach requires a different relation for each entity set and relationship in the hierarchy. The subtree approach requires one relation for each subtree, and the number of subtrees can be very large if the structure is at all complex. A root with n children would result in 2^n subtrees.

6.6.1.4.4.3 Comparison of Approaches for "isa" Relations – Issue #3

We generally like to minimize storage space and always prefer to avoid redundancy (repeating information.)

The subtree approach involves only one tuple for any entity and that tuple involves only attributes the "make sense" for that kind of entity, so this approach will require the minimum possible storage space.

The nulls approach also uses only one tuple per entity, but with this approach, the tuples are "long", involving (possibly) many nulls for attributes not appropriate for a given entity, so, if there are many entity sets with many different attributes, a large fraction of the storage space could be wasted.

The straight E/R approach will have several tuples for each entity, but only the key attributes will be repeated.

The straight E/R approach might require more storage space than the nulls approach or it might require less, depending on the structure of the database.

6.7 Chapter 6 Questions

6.7.1 True-False

6.7.1.1 Although almost all commercial database managers use the relational model, it is usually easier to start with a higher level model and then convert to a relational model.

6.7.1.2 Simplicity of concepts is a weakness when it comes to efficient implementation of design concepts, but can be a strength in preliminary design.

6.7.1.3 Attributes tend to be easier to implement than entity sets and/or relationships, but too many attributes can cause problems.

6.7.1.4 he relation for a weak entity set W must include not only the attributes of W, but also the key attributes from the supporting entity sets

6.7.1.5 When converting from E/R diagram to relational design, a supporting relationship from a weak entity set to a supporting entity set need not be converted to a relation

6.7.2 Multiple Choice

6.7.2.1 Which of the following models can represent multiway relationships
   a. E/R
   b. UML
   c. ODL
   d. all of the above
   e. none of the above

6.7.2.2 In order for R, a many-one relationship to some entity set F, to be a supporting relationship for E, the following condition must hold
   a. R must be a binary, many-one relationship from E to F
   b. R must have referential integrity from E to F
   c. For every E-entity, there must be exactly one existing F-entity related to it by R
   d. all of the above
   e. none of the above

6.7.2.3 In converting an E/R representation of an isa-hierarchy, there are several strategies that might be used. One is: For each possible subtree (that includes the root) create a relation whose schema include all attributes of entity sets in the subtree.
   This strategy is called
   a. Follow the E/R viewpoint
   b. Treat entities as objects belonging to a single class
   c. Use null values
   d. any of the above
   e. none of the above

6.7.3 Completion

    6.7.3.1 In the *entity-relationship model* (E/R model) the structure of data is represented graphically as an E/R diagram using three principal element types:
-    _____ sets
- Attributes
- Relationships

    6.7.3.2 In the *entity-relationship model* (E/R model) the structure of data is represented graphically as an E/R diagram using three principal element types:
- Entity sets
- Attributes
- _____

    6.7.3.3 _____ are *connections* between entity sets

6.7.3.4 An *E/R diagram* is a graph representing entity sets, attributes and relationships
- Elements of these types are represented by nodes of the graph and are distinguished by using different shapes for different kinds of entities
- Attributes are represented by _____

6.7.3.5 We connect an entity set to a subclass with a special kind of relationship called a(n)_____

6.7.3.6 A(n) _____ for an entity set E is a set K of one or more attributes such that two different entities in E cannot have identical values for the attributes in K

6.7.3.7 A referential-_____ constraint says that a value appearing in one context must also appear in another

6.7.3.8 It is *possible* for an entity set key to be composed of attributes, some or all of which belong to *another* entity set
- Such an entity set is called a(n) _____ *entity set*

6.7.3.9 If E is a weak entity set, then its key must consist of:
- Zero or more of its own attributes
- One or more key attributes that are reached by many-one relationships
- These many-one relationships are called _____ *relationships*

Chapter 7 High Level Database Models - UML

UML (Unified Modeling Language) was originally developed as a graphical notation for describing software designs in an object-oriented style. It has been extended (with some modifications) to make a notation for describing database designs.

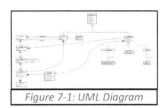

Figure 7-1: UML Diagram

UML has many of the same capabilities as the E/R model.

– UML also offers the ability to treat entity sets as true classes, with methods as well as data.

UML	E/R Model
Class	Entity set
Association	Binary relationship
Association Class	Attributes on a relationship
Subclass	Isa hierarchy
Aggregation	Many-one relationship
Composition	Many-one relationship with referential integrity

Figure 7-2:UML-E/R Terminologies

– UML and E/R use different terminology for the same concepts.

7.1 UML Classes

A class in UML is similar to an entity set in the E/R model, but the notation is somewhat different. The UML notation for a class is a box, divided into three parts:

At the top is the name of the class.

The middle section contains the class attributes, which are like class instance variables.

The bottom section is for methods.

Personnel
IDNumber PK
LastName
FirstName
SocSecNum
Gender
(This box for methods)

Figure 7-3: UML Class Diagram

Neither the E/R model nor the relational model support methods, but they appear in modern "object relational" DBMS's, where they are an important concept.

We will not include this section in any of our examples.

As with E/R entity sets, we can declare a key for a UML class. We follow each attribute in the key by the letters PK (standing for "*primary key*")

As with E/R diagrams, there is no convenient way to stipulate that alternative attributes are keys.

7.2 UML Associations

A binary relationship between classes is called an *association*.

There is no analog of multiway relationships in UML

What is called an *association* in UML is exactly what was described earlier as a *relationship*

An association consists of a collection of pairs of objects, one from each of the classes it connects.

7.2.1 Associations in Diagrams

We identify a UML *association* between two classes by drawing a line between them and giving the line a name.

Every such association has *constraints* on the number of objects in each class that can be connected with an object of the other class. We indicate these constraints by a label of the form "m..n" at each end of the line identifying the association.

– The meaning of this label is that each object at the other end is connected to at least m but no more than n objects at this end.

A symbol * in place of a number stands for infinity.

The pair m..* means there is no upper limit.

The symbol * alone would stand for the range 0..*

Such a symbol * would mean there are no constraints on the number of objects, that there could be *any* number of objects at the other end of the line.

Further, If there is *no* constraint label, then the label would be taken to be 1..1,

i.e. exactly 1

In Figure 7-4 we see "0..1" at the "Personnel" end of both of the id match associations. This would mean that a Personnel entry (a specific IDNumber) might (or might not) be associated with one (but no more than one) entry in the "Faculty" class, and/or with one (but no more than one) entry in the "Student" class. We see 1..1 at the "Faculty" end of "FacultyIDMatch" which means that each "Faculty" member will be associated with exactly one "Personnel" entry. Similarly, each "Student" is assigned exactly one "Personnel". entry.

The 0..* notation at the "Offices" end of the "OfficeOf" relation indicates that each office could be assigned any number of faculty members.

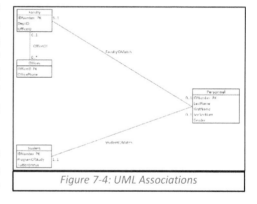

Figure 7-4: UML Associations

7.2.2 Self-Associations

An association can have both ends at the *same* class. We call such an association a *self-association*.

To distinguish between roles played the two objects in such an association, we assign names to both ends of the association.

For an example: Some courses cannot be taken without proper preparation (without having passed "prerequisite" courses.) In this example, it shows that a course can be a "PrerequisiteOf" zero or more other courses, and that any course might be a "SequelTo" (i.e. have as a prerequisite) any number of courses.

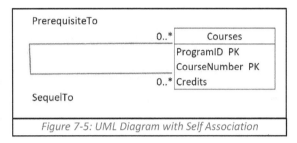

Figure 7-5: UML Diagram with Self Association

7.2.3 Association Classes

We can also attach attributes to a relation, just as we did with E/R relationships. In UML we do this by creating a new class (an *association class*) and attaching it to the center of the line representing the association.

The association class will have its own name, but the attributes are really properties of the association, so the class will not have a primary key. The class attributes will always be part of the tuple implementing the association.

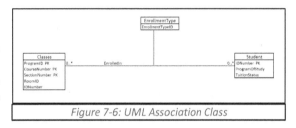

Figure 7-6: UML Association Class

7.3 Subclasses in UML

In UML any class can have a hierarchy of subclasses below it

UML permits a class to have any of four different kinds of subclasses. For a class C:

Subclasses of C can be complete or partial.

If every object in C is in some subclass, then they are complete, otherwise they are partial

Subclasses of C can be disjoint or overlapping.

If any object of C is in more than one subclass, then they are overlapping, otherwise they are disjoint.

In all of these cases, the primary key comes from the root class C.

To represent class-subclass associations we use a hollow arrow pointing to the superclass (the *root*.)

The *subclasses* are connected by a line feeding into the arrow line.

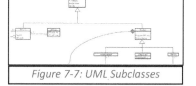

Figure 7-7: UML Subclasses

In Figure 7-7, putting entries "IDNumber   PK" in (sub)classes "Faculty and "Student" would be redundant, since the primary key of a subclass will be the same as that of the root class.

In this case the subclasses will (probably) be both *partial* (there will be "Personnel" who are neither students nor teachers) and disjoint (Faculty members are not Students and Students are not Faculty members.)

7.4 Aggregations and Compositions

There are two special notations for many-one relations that are used in place of numerical constraints. These notations are important in specifying how the UML diagram would be converted to a collection of relations. The notations are called *Aggregations* and *Compositions*:

Aggregations – A line between two classes that has an open diamond at one end.

Compositions – A line between two classes that has a solid diamond at one end.

7.4.1 Aggregations

The meaning of the open diamond [diagram] in an aggregation is essentially the same as that of being a 0..1 constraint.

An object from the class at the other end of the association line can be associated with no more than one object at the diamond end. It is not necessary to place a name on an aggregation, since, in practice, it will not end up being implemented as a relation.

7.4.2 Compositions

The meaning of the solid diamond [diagram] in a composition is the same as that of being a 1..1 constraint.

An object from the class at the other end of the association line must be associated with exactly one object from the class at the diamond end. With compositions, as with aggregations, it is generally not necessary to put a name on a composition, since in practice, it will not end up being implemented as a relation.

7.4.3 Example

In the example shown in (Figure 7-8):

As indicated above, compositions and aggregations do not normally require names, but, as we have *two* relations between "Department" and "Faculty" we need to assign them names in order to distinguish between them.

For the line connecting "Faculty" and "Offices", the "0..*" next to "Faculty" indicates that each office may be assigned to any number (including none) of faculty members. The empty diamond at the "Offices" end indicates that a faculty member is to be assigned no more than one office.

For the line labelled "MemberOf" between "Department" and "Faculty" the "0..*" next to "Faculty" indicates that a department might be assigned any number

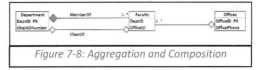

Figure 7-8: Aggregation and Composition

of faculty (including, possibly, no faculty at all.) The solid diamond at the "Department" end indicates that every faculty member must be assigned to exactly one department.

The two open diamonds at ends of the line labelled "DepartmentChair" indicate that each department will have no more than one chairman (a faculty member) and each faculty member will be a chairman of no more than one department.

7.5 From UML Diagrams to Relations

Many of the techniques for converting E/R diagrams into relations work equally well for creating relations from UML diagrams.

7.5.1 Classes to Relations

For each class (that is neither a subclass nor the initial class in an aggregation or composition) create a relation with the same name as the name of the class and with the same attributes as the UML class. Add primary keys of any many-one relations.

Personnel(<u>IDNumber</u>, LastName, FirstName, SocSecNum, DateOfBirth, Gender)

Sport(<u>SportID</u>)

HandicapAccommodation(<u>HandicapID</u>)

Offices(<u>OfficeID</u>, OfficePhone)

Classroom(<u>RoomID</u>, Capacity)

7.5.1.1 UML Subclasses to Relations

The conversion of *subclasses* (identified with the triangle symbol △) is subject to additional requirements that do not apply to regular classes. Primary among these is the requirement that the attributes of a subclass must include the primary key(s) of the superclass.

We have several subclasses in our example

> "Faculty" and "Student" are subclasses of "Personnel"

> "Handicapped", "NonCitizen" and "Athlete" are subclasses of "Student"

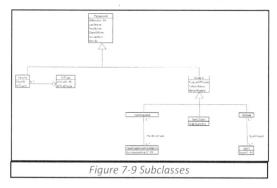

Figure 7-9 Subclasses

Since "Faculty" and "Student" are subclasses of "Personnel", each will have attribute "IDNumber" as (at least part of) its primary key.

> Faculty(<u>IDNumber</u>, DeptID, OfficeID)

> Student(<u>IDNumber</u>, ProgramOfStudy, TuitionStatus, HonorStudent)

Having identified the primary key for "Student", we can describe the relations for its subclasses "Handicapped", "Noncitizen" and "Athlete"

> Handicapped(<u>IDNumber</u>)

> Noncitizen(<u>IDNumber</u>, CountryOfOrigin)

> Athlete(<u>IDNumber</u>)

7.5.2 Associations to Relations

For each association (which is not a many-one relation), create a relation with the same name as the association. The attributes of the relation should be the key attributes of the two classes being "associated". Attribute names may need to be modified to avoid ambiguity. If there is an association class attached to the association, add the class attributes to those included in the relation.

7.5.2.1 Example

In our example UML diagram (Figure 7-1) the "HandicapType" and "SportPlayed" are many-many associations as is the "PrerequisiteOf-SequelTo" self association.

The derived relations[12] would be:

> HandicapType(<u>IDNumber</u>, <u>HandicapID</u>)

> SportPlayed(<u>IDNumber</u>, <u>SportID</u>)

> PrereqSequel(<u>PrereqID</u>, <u>SequelID</u>)

---

[12] Before we can program the "PrereqSequel" relation we will have to identify the primary key for the "Course" relation.

7.5.3 Representation of Many-One Associations

Any many-one association *could* be converted to a relation in the same way as we described for many-many associations, but it is simpler (and more efficient) to represent these associations using attributes with values identifying the "one" classes. These attributes will have as values, the primary key values of the class entries being identified (the classes on the "one" sides of the relations.)

7.5.3.1 From Aggregations and Compositions to Relations

The "many-one" associations in our example are all identified in the UML diagram using the diamond symbols described in section 7.4. Aggregations and compositions are specific types of many-one associations.

Recall that, if R is a many-one relation from an entity set E to another entity set F in an E/R diagram, then we can combine the relation for R with the relation for E, adding the key attributes from F (and any attributes of R) to those of E. We can represent the many-one associations from a UML diagram in exactly the same way.

The aggregation from "Faculty" to "Offices" is implemented by including an OfficeID" attribute in the "Faculty" relation and the "MemberOf" composition from "Faculty" to "Department" is implemented by including the "DeptID" attribute in "Faculty"

Faculty(<u>IDNumber</u>, **OfficeID**, **DeptID**)

The one-one aggregation "DepartmentChair" between "Department" and "Faculty" could be implemented either with an attribute in relation "Department" or in Relation "Faculty". Neither implementation enforces the one-one nature of the association and an external constraint will be necessary for this.

Since there are many fewer departments than there are faculty members, putting a "ChairOfDepartment" attribute in the "Faculty" relation would result in many null values in the "Faculty" table and inefficient utilization of storage space. One can assume, on the other hand, that most departments will have a chairperson, so a "ChairIDNumber" attribute in the "Department" relation will result in very few null values.

Department(<u>DeptID</u>, **ChairIDNumber**)

7.6 The UML Analog of Weak Entity Sets

We can use composition in UML as we used "supporting relationships" in the E/R model to describe weak entities and weak relationships. We attach a box with the letters "PK" to the "weak" class.

We convert these weak structures to relations exactly the same way that we did the weak structures in E/R models.

Program(<u>ProgramID</u>, DeptID)

Course(<u>ProgramID</u>, <u>CourseID</u>, Credits)

Classes(<u>ProgramID</u>,<u>CourseID</u>,<u>SectionNumber</u>,TeacherIDNumber,RoomID)

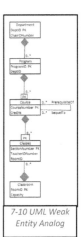

7-10 UML Weak Entity Analog

7.7 Object Definition Language

ODL (Object Definition Language) is a text based language for specifying the structure of databases in object-oriented terms.

The *class* is the central concept in ODL

Classes have *names, attributes* and *methods*

7.7.1 ODL Class Declarations

A class declaration in ODL will have the following format:

```
class <name> {
        <list of properties>
};
```

The list of properties might include attributes, relationships, structured types, collection types and/or methods.

Relationships (analogous to associations in UML or relationships in the E/R model) are not an independent concept in ODL. They are embedded within classes as properties of the classes.

7.7.2 ODL Attributes

An attribute is represented in a declaration for its class by the keyword attribute, the type of the attribute and the name of the attribute.

Example:

Class Office {

attribute string OfficeID;

attribute string OfficePhone;

};

In ODL, attributes need not be simple types. The ODL type system allows us to form structured types and collection types.

7.7.2.1 Enumeration Types

An enumeration type is a list of symbolic constants.

An enumeration type must have a name so that it can be used elsewhere to refer to the same data type.

Example with enum:

```
Class Personnel {
    attribute string IDNumber;
    attribute string LastName;
    attribute string FirstNname;
    attribute string SocSecNum;
    attribute enum Genders
        {M,F} PGender;
};
```

In this example "Genders" is the name of an enumeration type that could be used in other classes while "PGender" is the name of the attribute of an individual "Personnel" entry.

Example applying the user defined type in another class definition:

```
Class Student {
    attribute string IDNumber;
    attribute string ProgramOfStudy;
    attribute string TuitionStatus;
    attribute Genders StuGender;
};
```

7.7.2.2 Structure Types

In general, one can define *structure* types in ODL using the keyword "Struct" and curly braces around a list of field names and their types. As with enumerations, structure types must have names which can be used to refer to the same structure types in other class definitions.

Example with structure type:

```
Class Personnel {
    attribute string IDNumber;
    attribute string SocSecNum;
    attribute enum Genders
        {M,F} PGender;
    attribute Struct Names
        {
            string FirstName;
            string LastName
        } PNames
};
```

In this example a structure type is defined. The name of the type is "Names" " and has fields named "FirstName" and "LastName", both of which are of type string. The "Names" type can be referenced by other class definitions and such references would not require redefinition. The attribute of type "Names" in the "Personnel" class is called "PNames".

Example with references to externally defined types:

Class Faculty {

    attribute string IDNumber;

    attribute Names FacultyNames;

    attribute string OfficeID;

    attribute Genders FacultyGender;

};

This class declaration assumes that types "Genders" and "Names" were defined in some other class. (In this example they were defined in class "Personnel".)

7.7.3 ODL Relationships

ODL relationships are defined in classes, using the keyword "*relationship*".

The definition of a relationship will include the name of a data type, and a name for the relationship.

Typically, the *type* describes what a single object of the class is connected/related to:

the name of another class if the relation is one-one or many-one,

the name of a kind of *collection* if the relation is one-many or many-many

There are several kinds of collections available. Among them are *sets*, *lists* and *bags*.

The ODL relationships statement also supports an "*inverse*" extension identifying an associated relationship in another class.

7.7.3.1 ODL Relationships Example 1

Recall that faculty members are assigned offices (with telephones) so there is a (many one) relationship from "Faculty" to "Office".

class Faculty {

    attribute string IDNumber;

    attribute Names FacultyNames;

    attribute Genders FacultyGender;

    relationship Office TeachersOffice
        inverse Office::TeachersAssigned;

};

This "Faculty declaration establishes a relationship, each faculty member associated with one "Office" entity (association identified by attribute name "TeachersOffice"), but the "inverse" clause creates a requirement that the "Office" class must include a relationship identified as "TeachersAssigned".

7.7.3.2 ODL Relationships Example 2

The relationship "TeachersAssigned from "Office" to "Faculty" specified in the "Faculty" class in 7.7.3.1 is different from "TeachersOffice" from "Faculty" to "Office". An individual office is not necessarily assigned to just one teacher. An office will typically be shared by a collection (a *set*) of faculty members. The "TeachersOffice" relation is many-one but the "TeachersAssigned" relation is one many.

```
class Office {

    attribute string OfficeID;

    attribute string OfficePhone;

    relationship Set<Faculty> TeachersAssigned
        inverse Faculty::TeachersOffice

};
```

7.7.3.3 The "inverse" declaration in an ODL Relationship

If the "TeachersOffice" attribute value for faculty member x happens to be the identifier of office y, then we would naturally assume that the "TeachersAssigned" value for office y should include faculty member x, and, conversely, if the faculty member b is in the TeachersAssigned set of values for office a, then the TeachersOffice value for a should be office b.

The "*inverse*" keyword specifies this precise type of interrelationship between two relations.

Note that it is normally necessary to identify the *class* in which the other relation is defined. To do this, we use the double colon notation … *class :: relationship*.

A pair of inverse relationships can be many-many, one-one or many-one in either direction. The type declarations of the pair relationships allow us to determine which.

If we have a many-many relationship between classes C and D, then the type relationship in C is Set<D> and that in class D is Set<C>

If we have a many-one relationship from C to D, then the type of relation in C is just D while that in D is Set<C>

If the relationship is one-one, then the type in C is D and the type in D is C.

7.7.4 Types in ODL

ODL offers the database designer a system for constructing data types that is similar to that found in many modern languages (including C.)

A *type system* is built from *basis types* using several recursive rules for constructing complex types from simpler types.

7.7.4.1 ODL Basis Types

The basis types are either primitive types or names of types defined elsewhere in the collection.

Primitive types are: Integer, float, character, character string, boolean and enumerations

7.7.4.2 ODL Type Constructors

The basis types can be combined into structured types using the following constructors:
Set; Bag; List; Array; Dictionary; Struct

The first five of these:

  Set, Bag, List, Array and Dictionary,

are called *collection types.*

7.7.4.2.1 Set

  If T is a type, then Set<T> is the type whose values are finite collections of objects
  of type T.

7.7.4.2.2 Bag

  If T is a type, then Bag<T> is the type whose values are finite "bags" (multisets) of
  objects of type T.

  If A and B are objects of type T, then {A, B} and {A, B, B} would be the same
  set but not the same *bag*.

7.7.4.2.3 List

  If T is a type, then List<T> is the type whose values are finite lists (*sequences*) of 0
  or more objects of type T.

  {A,B,B} and {B,A,B} are the same *set* and the same *bag* but not the same *list*.

7.7.4.2.4 Array

  If T is a type and I is an integer, then Array<T,i> denotes the type whose objects
  are arrays of length i of objects of type T.

7.7.4.2.5 Dictionary

  If T an S are types, then Dictionary<T,S> denotes a type whose objects are finite
  sets of pairs. Each pair an object of the *key* type T and an object of the *range* type
  S.

  The dictionary may not contain two pairs with the same key value.

7.7.4.2.6 Structures

  If T1, T2, …, Tn are names of types and F1, F2, …, Fn are names of fields, then
      Struct N {T1 F1, T2 F2, … ,Tn Fn}
  denotes the type named N whose elements are structures with n fields.

  Field number j is named Fj and has type Tj

  Recall in an earlier example, class "Personnel" has attribute PNames
      Struct Names
      {
          string FirstName;
          string LastName
      } PNames

7.7.4.2.7 Rules for Using Types

There are different rules about which types may be associated with attributes and which types can be used with relationships.

Attributes: The type of an attribute is built starting with primitive type(s) and applying constructors.

Relationships: The type of a relationship is either a class type or a collection type constructor applied to a class type. Neither primitive types nor "Struct"s can be used for relationships.

7.7.5 Subclasses in ODL

We can declare a class C to be a *subclass* of another class D by following the name C in its declaration with the keyword "*extends*" and naming the class D

– In this case, the class C inherits all of the properties of D and may (probably will) have some of its own.

Example:

class Handicapped extends Student {

    relationship Set<HandicapAccommodations> StudentAccommodations
        inverse HandicapAccommodations::StudentsAccommodated;

};

class ForeignStudent extends Student {

    attribute string OriginCountry;

};

With this structure, a handicapped student and/or a foreign student will have attributes IDNumber, Gender, FirstName and LastName. A foreign student will have a string attribute named OriginCountry.

Note that this structure also implies that class "HandicapAccommodations" must also have a relationship "StudentsAccommodated

class HandicapAccommodations {

    string AccommodationID;

    relationship Set<Handicapped> StudentsAccommodated
        inverse Handicapped::StudentAccommodations;

};

7.7.5.1 Multiple Subclasses in ODL

Sometimes we need a class to be a subclass of two or more classes at the same time. ODL does, in fact, support this kind of structure.

We may follow the keyword *extends* by a colon separated list of class names:

    class HandicappedForeignStudent extends HandicappedStudent : ForeignStudent;

Note that when there is multiple inheritance, there is potential for a class to inherit two properties with the same name.

The way such conflicts are resolved is implementation dependent.

7.7.6 Keys in ODL

The declaration of keys for a class is optional in ODL. We may declare one or more attributes to be a key for a class by using the keyword *key* or *keys* (either one, the two are equivalent) followed by the attribute or attributes.

The key declaration itself must be enclosed in parentheses

```
class Office (key OfficeID) {
    attribute string OfficeID;
    attribute string OfficePhone;
    relationship Set<Faculty> TeachersAssigned
        inverse Faculty::TeachersOffice
};
```

If there is more than one attribute in the key, they must be enclosed in parentheses.

```
class Courses (key (Course, Program)) {
    attribute string Course;
    attribute string Program;
    attribute integer Credits;
    relationship Set<Classes> SectionsOf
        inverse Classes::CourseFor;
}
```

Unlike E/R or UML, with ODL, more than one key can be specified.

```
class Personnel key (IDNumber, SocSecNum) {
    attribute string IDNumber;
    attribute string SocSecNum;
    attribute enum Genders
        {M,F} PGender;
    attribute Struct Names {
        string FirstName;
        string LastName
    } PNames
};
```

The ODL standard also allows properties other than attributes to appear as keys. We can obtain an effect similar to that of weak entity sets by declaring a many one relationship to be (part of) a key.

```
class Classes (key (CourseFor, Section)) {
    attribute string Section;
    relationship Courses CourseFor
        inverse Courses::SectionsOf;
};
```

High Level Database Models – UML and ODL

7.7.7 Full College Database Structure in ODL

```
class Personnel key (IDNumber,
SocSecNum) {
    attribute string IDNumber;
    attribute string SocSecNum;
    attribute enum Genders
        {M,F} PGender;
    attribute Struct Names
    {   string FirstName;
        string LastName
    } PNames
};
class Faculty extends Personnel {
    relationship Office TeachersOffice
        inverse
Office::TeachersAssigned;
    relationship Department
MemberOf
        inverse
Department::DepartmentMembers;
};
class Office key (OfficeID) {
    attribute string OfficeID;
    attribute string OfficePhone;
    relationship Set<Faculty>
TeachersAssigned
        inverse
Faculty::TeachersOffice;
};
class Department key (DeptID) {
    attribute string DeptID;
    relationship Set<Faculty>
DepartmentMembers
        inverse Faculty::MemberOf;
    attribute Faculty
DepartmentChair;
};
class Program key(ProgramID) {
    attribute string ProgramID;
    relationship Department DeptID;
};
class Course extends Program key
(ProgramID, CourseNumber) {
    attribure string CourseNumber;
    attribute integer credits;
    relationship Set<Course>
PrerequsiteOf
        inverse Course::SequelTo;
    relationship <Set<Course>
SequelTo

};
```

```
        inverse
Course::PrerequisiteOf;
};
class Classes extends Course
        key(ProgramID, CourseNumber,
SecionNumber) {
    attribute string SectionNumber;
    attribute Faculty Teacher;
    attribute Classroom
RoomAssigned;
    relationship Set<EnrolledIn>
Roster
        inverse
EnrolledIn::ClassOfEnrollment;
};
class Classroom key(RoomID){
    attribute string RoomID;
    attribute integer Capacity;
};
class Student extends Personnel {
    attribute string ProgramOfStudy;
    attribute string TuitionStatus;
    relationship Set<EnrolledIn>
Enrollment
        inverse EnrolledIn::StudentID;
};
class EnrolledIn {
    attribute string EnrollmentType;
    relationship Classes
ClassOfEnrollment
        inverse Classes::Roster;
    relationship Student StudentID
        inverse Student::Enrollment;
};
class Handicapped extends Student {
    relationship
Set<HandicapAccommodation>
HandicapType;
};
class NonCitizen extends Student {
    attribute string OriginCountry;
};
class Athlete {
    relationship Set<Sport>
SportPlayed;
};
class Sport {
    attribute string SportID;
```

7.7.8 Relational Databases from ODL

ODL was originally intended as the data definition part of a language standard for object oriented DBMS's and there have been some attempts to implement such a system.

It is also possible to look at ODL as a high level design notation from which we would derive a relational schema. Much of the process is quite similar to what we did with E/R diagrams and UML but some aspects of ODL create new and significant problems. Among these problems are:

Although entity sets must have keys, ODL classes are not required to have keys.

Attributes in E/R, UML and the relational model are required to be of primitive types, but there is no such constraint for ODL attributes.

Because of these problems, if one wants to use ODL in the design of a system intended for a relational database system, then one should, at the very least, limit the complexity of the types of attributes one uses.

High Level Database Models – UML and ODL

7.8 Chapter 7 Questions

7.8.1 True-False

7.8.1.1 UML (Unified Modeling Language) was originally developed as a graphical notation for describing database designs. It has been extended (with some modifications) to a notation for describing software designs in an object oriented style.

7.8.1.2 In UML, if there is no constraint label at one end of an association, then that label is taken to be 1..1

7.8.1.3 The meaning of an open diamond in an aggregation is similar to a 0..1 constraint.

7.8.1.4 The meaning of a solid diamond in a composition is similar to a 0..1 constraint.

7.8.1.5 In a UML system it is possible that we might have more information than in an E/R system.

7.8.1.6 Relationships (analogous to associations in UML or relationships in the E/R model) are not an independent concept in ODL. They are embedded within classes as properties of the classes.

7.8.1.7 The declaration of keys for a class is optional in ODL

7.8.2 Multiple Choice

7.8.2.1 The UML term for what in an E/R diagram would be called a binary relationship is:
   a. class
   b. association
   c. subclass
   d. any of the above
   e. none of the above

7.8.2.2 In a UML diagram, a line between two classes that has an open diamond at one end represents a(n)
   a. association
   b. binding
   c. aggregation
   d. composition
   e. none of the above

7.8.2.3 In a UML diagram, a line between two classes that has a solid diamond at one end represents a(n)
   a. association
   b. binding
   c. aggregation
   d. composition
   e. none of the above

7.8.2.4 If we have a _____ relationship from C to D, then the type of relation in C is D while that in D is C
   a. many-many
   b. many-one
   c. one-one
   d. any of the above
   e. none of the above

7.8.2.5 If we have a _____ relationship from C to D, then the type of relation in C is just D while that in D is Set<C>
a. many-many
b. many-one
c. one-one
d. any of the above
e. none of the above

7.8.3 Completion

7.8.3.1 A(n) ___ in UML is similar to an entity set in the E/R model.

7.8.3.2 We can attach attributes to a relation, just as we did with E/R relationships
In UML we create a new class (a(n) _____ class) and attach it to the center of the line representing the association.

7.8.3.3 UML permits a class C to have any of four different kinds of subclasses:
–Subclasses of C can be complete or partial.
–Subclasses of C can be disjoint or _____

7.8.3.4 We can use composition in UML as we used "_____ relationships" in the E/R model to describe weak entities and weak relationships.

7.8.3.5 ODL offers the database designer a system for constructing _____ types that is similar to that found in many modern languages.

7.8.3.6 The five constructors - Set, Bag, List, Array and Dictionary - are called _____ types.

Chapter 8 Algebraic and Logical Query Languages

In chapter 2, we introduced relational algebra, an algebraic programming language. In Chapter 7 we introduced the concept of a *bag* (Section 7.7.4.2.2).

In this chapter we will extend the set based algebra from chapter 2 to include the chapter 7 bags.

Bags generally better reflect the way the relational model is implemented in practice.

We will also add a few extra operations that are useful in database programming.

8.1 Relational Operations on Bags

We will be considering relations that are *bags* (multisets.)

(The same tuple can appear more than once in a relation.)

Implementing this interpretation requires a number of changes in the definitions of some of the relational operations.

A	B
1	2
3	4
1	2
1	2

Figure 8.1 Relation with Tuples Appearing Multiple Times

8.1.1 Relational Operations on Bags: Why must we use Bags?

Commercial DBMS's generally implement relations as bags rather than sets, so if we are to make use of such systems, we must understand bags.

8.1.1.1 Relational Operations on Bags: Why do DBMS's use Bags?

Some relational operations are much more efficient as bags.

If we compute the *union* of two relations as bags, we simply copy one and then add all the tuples in the other. There is no need to eliminate duplicates.

When we project relations as sets, we need to compare each projected tuple with the other tuples to avoid duplication. If we intend a bag as a projection output, we simply add the projections of each of the tuples to the result, without comparing them to previously projected tuples.

8.1.1.2 Relational Operations on Bags Another Reason for using Bags

Another motivation for relations as bags is that there are some situations where the expected answer can only be obtained if we use bags.

Example: Suppose that we want to compute the average of the A-components of the relation in Figure 8.2.

As a set, the projection of the A component has two values, 1 and 3 so the average would be 2, but as a bag, the projection has four values, {1,3,1,1} and their average would be 1.5

A	B	C
1	2	5
3	4	6
1	2	7
1	2	8

Figure 8.2

Query Languages

8.1.2 Relational Operations on Bags: Unions, Intersections and Differences:

These three operations have somewhat different definitions for bags than they do for sets.

Suppose R and S are bags (of tuples) and that the tuple t appears m times in R and n times in S. (Note that m and/or n might be zero.)

In the bag union $R \cup S$ the tuple t appears m+n times.

In the bag intersection $R \cap S$ the tuple t appears min(m,n) times.

In the bag difference R-S the tuple t will appear max(0,n-m) times.

Example: Let R be the relation Figure 8.1 This relation is a bag in which the tuple (1,2) appears 3 times and the tuple (3,4) appears once.

Let S be the relation in Figure 8.3 (also a bag.)

A	B
1	2
3	4
4	4
5	6

Figure 8.3

The relations R and S both have the same number of attributes (two), with the same names, A and B, and so it is possible to form their union $R \cup S$, intersection $R \cap S$ and difference R-S

The bag union $R \cup S$ is a bag in which:

(1,2) appears 4 times

(3,4) appears 3 times

(5,6) appears once

A	B
1	2
1	2
1	2
1	2
3	4
3	4
3	4
5	6

R∪S

The bag intersection $R \cap S$ is a bag in which:

(1,2) appears once

(3,4) appears once

A	B
1	2
3	4

R∩S

The bag difference R-S is a bag in which:

(1,2) appears twice

A	B
1	2
1	2

R-S

8.1.3 Relational Operations on Bags: Projections of Bags:

In calculating a projection, each tuple is processed individually.

If R is the bag of Figure 8.2

The projection $\pi_A(R)$ is {1,3,1,1}

The projection $\pi_{AB}(R)$ is the relation shown at the right:

A	B
1	2
3	4
1	2
1	2

$\pi_{AB}(R)$

8.1.4 Relational Operations on Bags: Selection of Bags:

To apply a *selection* to a bag, we apply the selection condition to each tuple independently.

We do NOT eliminate duplicate tuples in the result.

If R is the relation in Figure 8.2, the result of applying the bag-selection $\sigma_{C \geq 6}(R)$ results in the bag displayed at the right.

A	B	C
3	4	6
1	2	7
1	2	8

$\sigma_{C \geq 6}(R)$

118

8.1.5 Relational Operations on Bags: Products of Bags:

The rule for products of bags is the same as for sets, with the (obvious) difference that duplicate results are not removed.

Example Bag Product:

A	B	B	C	A	R.B	S.B	C
1	2	2	3	1	2	2	3
1	2			1	2	4	5
R		4	5	1	2	4	5
		4	5	1	2	2	3
		S		1	2	4	5
				1	2	4	5
				R×S			

Figure 8-4

8.1.6 Relational Operations on Bags: Joins of Bags:

The *joins* of bags are computed in exactly the same way that the corresponding joins are computed for sets. Each tuple of one relation is compared with each tuple of the other to determine whether or not this couple joins successfully. If the tuples do join successfully, the combination is placed in the result.

Example Natural Join:
Computing the natural join R⋈S of the two relations R and S in Figure 8-5, we note the B component of each (1,2) in R matches the B component of (2,3) in S.

A	B	B	C	A	B	C
1	2	2	3	1	2	3
1	2	4	5	1	2	3
R		4	5	R⋈S		
		S				

Figure 8-5

Example Theta Join:
The theta join $R \bowtie_{R.B<S.B} S$ of these relations R and S produces the relation displayed in Figure 8-6.

A	R.B	S.B	C
1	2	4	5
1	2	4	5
1	2	4	5
1	2	4	5
$R \bowtie_{R.B<S.B} S$			

Figure 8-6

8.2 Extended Relational Operations

In Chapter 2 we introduced the classical relational algebra.

In section (8.1) we introduced modifications necessary for dealing with *bags* of tuples rather than *sets* of tuples.

The information in these two sections serves as the basis for most modern query languages.

Languages such as SQL, however, have included several additional operations that have proved quite important in applications. A full treatment of relational operations must include some of these additional operators.

8.2.1 The *duplicate-elimination* Operator

Sometimes we need an operator that converts a bag into a set. The duplicate elimination operator δ fills that need. It simply removes any tuples that duplicate other tuples in the relation and produces a (new) relation in which the collection of tuples forms a set rather than a bag.

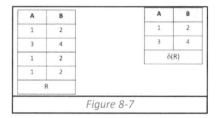

Figure 8-7

8.2.2 Aggregation Operators

Aggregation operators (sums, averages, …) are not operations of relational algebra but are utilized in conjunction with the grouping operator (described next). The aggregation operators apply to attributes (columns.)

As an example, the *SUM* operator will produce the number that is the sum of all the numbers in one column.

There are several such (aggregation) operators that apply to collections (sets or bags) of numbers or strings. These operators are used to summarize or "aggregate" the values in a column of a relation. That is why they are called *aggregate* operators.

The standard[13] aggregate operators are:

1. SUM produces the sum of the entries in a column with numerical values.

2. AVG produces the average of the entries in a column with numerical values.

3. MIN and MAX produce the smallest/largest value in a column with entries that can be compared in "size" or order.

4. COUNT produces the number of (not necessarily distinct) entries in a column.

---

[13] There is some variation in operators available in the different query languages.

Some examples obtained applying these aggregates to relation R in Figure 8-8 are:

A	B
1	2
3	4
1	2
1	2

R

Figure 8-8

SUM(B) = 10

AVG(A) = 1.5

MIN(A) = 1

MAX(B) = 4

COUNT(A) = 4

8.2.3 The Grouping Operator

The grouping operator γ is an operator that allows us to combine the effects of grouping and aggregation.

Often we do not want the average (or some other aggregate) of ALL the entries in an entire column. We might, instead, need to consider the tuples of a relation in groups, determined by some condition (Usually based on values in one or more other columns.)

Grouping of tuples according to their value in one or more attributes has the effect of *partitioning* the tuples of a relation, dividing them up into "*groups*".

Such grouping supports aggregation, which can then be applied to columns *within* each group and gives us the ability to express a number of queries impossible to express in classical relational algebra.

The operator γ uses a subscript that is a list L of elements, each of which is either:

An *attribute* if it is the relation to which the operator is applied.

In this case, the attribute is one of the attributes according to which R is to be subdivided. The attribute is referred to as a *grouping attribute*.

An *aggregation operator* that will be applied to an attribute of the relation.

In order to provide a name for the attribute corresponding to this attribute in the result, an arrow and a new name can be appended to the aggregation.

The underlying attribute is called an *aggregated attribute*

The operation $\gamma_L(R)$ produces a relation constructed as follows:

Partition the tuples of R into groups. each group consisting of all tuples having one particular assignment of values to the grouping attributes in the list L (if there are no grouping attributes the entire relation R is one group.)

For each group, produce one tuple consisting of:

The grouping attributes values for that group and

The aggregations over all members of that group for the aggregated attributes on list L.

Example: Suppose that our example college wants to determine the total number credits assigned to each of its teachers:

In the college database we might have a relation with schema

Classes(

ProgramID,

CourseNumber, ,

SectionNumber,

TeacherIDNumber,

RoomID

)

and a relation with schema

Course(

ProgramID,

CourseNumber,

Credits

)

The natural join Classes⋈Courses will have attribute list:

(

ProgramID,

CourseNumber,

SectionNumber,

TeacherIDNumber,

RoomID,

Credits

)

We must group together the classes/sections with the same TeacherIDNumber values, and then sum the course credits of each of the classes in each group:

The operation

$\gamma_{TeacherIDNumber,SUM(Credits)\rightarrow AssignedLoad}(Classes\bowtie Courses)$ might produce a table like that of Figure 8-9. (presumably with many more Teachers represented.)

TeacherIDNumber	AssignedLoad
...	...
876221234	8
882475631	12
...	...

Figure 8-9

8.2.4 Extended Projection

Extended projection gives additional power to the projection operator π.

In addition to projecting out some columns, in its *generalized* form, the projection operator π supports the output of the results of computations involving the columns of its argument relation.

When we introduced the projection operator $\pi_L(R)$ earlier, L was a list of attributes of R.

We now augment the definition of $\pi_L(R)$ by extending it, allowing the subscript L to include elements of the following types:

A single attribute of R

An expression of the form x→y where x and y are names for attributes

> For this type of element, the expression x→y in the list asks that values from the attribute named x be listed under a column labelled y in the projection relation.

An expression of the form E→z where E is an expression involving attributes of R, constants, arithmetic operators and string operators and z is a name for an attribute with values that result from the calculations described by the expression E

The result of applying $\pi_L(R)$ is computed by substituting the component values for each of the corresponding values of L and applying any operators.

Example:

> Let R be the relation shown in Figure 8-10:
>
> The result of applying the expression
>
> $$\pi_{A,B+C\rightarrow X}(R)$$
>
> would produce the relation shown.

A	B	C
0	1	2
0	1	2
3	4	5

R

A	X
0	3
0	3
3	9

$\pi_{A,B+C\rightarrow X}(R)$

Figure 8-10

For another example:

> When the operator
>
> $$\pi_{B-A\rightarrow X,C-B\rightarrow Y}(R)$$
>
> is applied to the relation R from Figure 8-10, the result would be as shown here in Figure 8-11

X	Y
1	1
1	1
1	1

$\pi_{B-A\rightarrow X,C-B\rightarrow Y}(R)$

Figure 8-11

8.2.5 The Sorting Operator

The *sorting operator* τ turns a relation into a list of tuples sorted according to one or more attributes. There are many contexts in which we want the tuples in a relation to appear in an order determined by (some of) the attributes.

> Possibly to make information easier to find.
>
> Possibly to make certain processes more efficient.

If R is a relation and L is a list of attributes of R, then the expression $\tau_L(R)$ is the relation with all of the tuples of R but sorted in the order indicated by L.

> If L is the list $A_1, A_2, \ldots, A_n$, then $\tau_L(R)$ sorts the tuples according to their values in A_1. Tuples with the same values for A_1 are sorted according to their values in A_2. Tuples with the same values in both A_1 and A_2 are sorted according to their values in A_3, …
>
> Tuples that agree on all of the attributes in L would be arranged arbitrarily.

Assuming that R is the relation shown below in Figure 8-12, then $\tau_{B,D}(R)$ would produce the second relation shown:

A	B	C	D
1	2	4	5
1	3	5	4
3	1	4	5
2	2	6	2
R			

A	B	C	D
3	1	4	5
2	2	6	2
1	2	4	5
1	3	5	4
$\tau_{B,D}(R)$			

Figure 8-12

8.2.6 The Outerjoin Operator

The *outerjoin* operator is a variant of the join operator that avoids losing information from *dangling* tuples.

Dangling tuples are tuples that fail to match any tuple of the other relation.

With the (natural) *join* operator $\bowtie$, it is possible for tuples to be "dangling"

In the relations U and V below, the B,C attribute values of tuples (4,5,6) and (7,8,9) from relation U fail to match any B,C attribute values in V and, so they are "dangling". They are not represented in the natural join U$\bowtie$V. The B,C values of (6,7,9) in V fail to match any B,C values in U, so (6,7,9) is also dangling, and these values are not represented in the natural join U$\bowtie$V.

A	B	C
1	2	3
4	5	6
7	8	9
U		

B	C	D
2	3	10
2	3	11
6	7	9
V		

A	B	C	D
1	2	3	10
1	2	3	11
U$\bowtie$V			

Figure 8-13

A modified version of the join operation, the *outerjoin*, $\overset{o}{\bowtie}$, eliminates dangling tuples by "padding" them with *null* values so that they can be represented in the output. The outerjoin makes it possible for information in dangling tuples to be retained in the join relation. Entries with the information from the dangling tuples are added to the output relation, with the null character (which we represent with the symbol $\perp$) in the attributes that are not from the relation of the dangling tuple.

Example: In Figure 8-14, the tuples (4,5,6) and (7,8,9) from relation U are dangling, as is tuple (6,7,9) from relation V.

Attribute D appears in the attribute list for the join, but is not an attribute of relation U, so the outerjoin operation pads the dangling tuples from U with ⊥ in the D attribute. Similarly, A is an attribute from the join which does not appear in the attribute list of relation V, and so the dangling tuple from V is padded with ⊥ in the A attribute to create an entry in the outerjoin.

A	B	C		B	C	D		A	B	C	D
1	2	3		2	3	10		1	2	3	10
4	5	6		2	3	11		1	2	3	11
7	8	9		6	7	9		4	5	6	⊥
								7	8	9	⊥
								⊥	6	7	9`

U · V · U ⋈ V

Figure 8-14

8.2.7 There are several variations of the outerjoin operation:

The left outerjoin $\overset{o}{\bowtie}_L$ in which only tuples from the left relation are padded with ⊥.

A	B	C	D
1	2	3	10
1	2	3	11
4	5	6	⊥
7	8	9	⊥

The right outerjoin $\overset{o}{\bowtie}_R$ in which only tuples from the right relation are padded with ⊥

A	B	C	D
1	2	3	10
1	2	3	11
⊥	6	7	9

In addition, all three have theta-join analogs, where first a theta-join is computed, and then any missing tuples are padded with ⊥ and added to the resulting relation.

8.3 Chapter 8 Questions

8.3.1 True-False

8.3.1.1 Sets generally reflect the way the relational model is implemented in practice better than do bags.

8.3.1.2 Using bags the same tuple can appear only once in a relation.

8.3.1.3 Commercial DBMS's implement relations as sets rather than bags.

8.3.1.4 One motivation for relations as bags is that there are some situations where the expected answer can only be obtained if we use bags.

8.3.1.5 Unions, intersections and differences have slightly different definitions for bags than they do for sets.

8.3.1.6 The joins of bags are computed in a slightly different way than they are computed for sets.

8.3.2 Multiple Choice

8.3.2.1 The bag union $R \cup S$ is a bag in which the tuple (5,6) appears _____ times

A	B
1	2
3	4
1	2
1	2
R	

A	B
1	2
3	4
3	4
5	6
S	

a. 1
b. 2
c. 3
d. 4
e. none of the above

8.3.2.2 The bag intersection $R \cap S$ is a bag in which (1,2) appears _____ times

A	B
1	2
3	4
1	2
1	2
R	

A	B
1	2
3	4
3	4
5	6
S	

a. 1
b. 2
c. 3
d. 4
e. none of the above

8.3.2.3 The *duplicate-elimination* operator _____ turns a bag into a set by eliminating all but one copy of each tuple.
   a. δ
   b. τ
   c. g
   d. σ
   e. none of the above

8.3.2.4 *Extended projection* gives additional power to the operator _____. In addition to projecting out some columns, in its generalized form, the operator can perform computations involving the columns of its argument relation to produce new columns.
   a. δ
   b. τ
   c. γ
   d. σ
   e. none of the above

8.3.2.5 The *sorting* operator _____ turns a relation into a list of tuples sorted according to one or more attributes.
   a. δ
   b. τ
   c. γ
   d. σ
   e. none of the above

8.3.3 Completion

8.3.3.1 In this chapter we will extend the set based algebra to _____.

– This better reflects the way the relational model is implemented in practice.

8.3.3.2 _____ operators (sums, averages, …) are not operations of relational algebra but are used by the grouping operator (described next). These operators apply to attributes (columns.)

8.3.3.3 The standard aggregate operators are:
   • _____ produces the sum of the entries in a column with numerical values
   • AVG produces the average of the entries in a column with numerical values
   • MIN and MAX produces the smallest/largest value in a column with entries that can be compared in "size" or order
   • COUNT produces the number of (not necessarily distinct) entries in a column.

8.3.3.4 If the operator γ uses a subscript that is a list L of elements, each of which is an *attribute* then the attributes are referred to as _____ *attributes*

9.0 The Database Language SQL

The most widely used DBMS's use a language called SQL[14] to query and modify their databases. SQL serves both as a data manipulation language and as a data definition language. Because it is so widely used, it tends to serve as a standard for many database systems.

The part of SQL that supports queries is fairly close to the extended relational algebra as described in chapter 8 but also includes statements for modifying the database.

There are many different dialects of SQ:

– ANSI SQL

– An updated standard adopted in 1992 called SQL-92 or SQL2

– SQL-99 (also called SQL3) which extends SQL2 with object relational features and some new capabilities

– A collection of extensions to SQL-99 collectively called SQL:2003

– There are also versions of SQL produced by individual major DBMS vendors

> These conform to ANSI SQL and generally to SQL2, although each has extensions beyond SQL2. They generally include some, but not all of SQL-99 and SQL:2003.

9.1 Simple Queries in SQL

An SQL query creates a new (temporary) relation based on the contents of existing relations in the database.

The simplest form of query in SQL creates a relation consisting of those tuples in one relation that satisfy some condition.

> Analogous to a *selection* in relational algebra.

These *simple* queries (and, in fact, *most* SQL queries) use the keywords SELECT, FROM and WHERE

> Note that SQL is *not* case sensitive. Our use of uppercase letters in keywords and camelback notation in attribute names is intended to improve readability. It has no effect on program execution.

> String interpretation, however, (as in values of string attributes) IS case sensitive.

---

[14] Officially pronounced "sequel" but frequently "ess que ell"

In many (most?) of the examples in this chapter we will be referencing the following schemas of an example College database:

Personnel(IDNumber, SocSecNum, LastName, FirstName, DateOfBirth, Gender)
Faculty(IDNumber, OfficeID, DeptID)
Offices(OfficeID, OfficePhone)
Student(IDNumber, ProgramOfStudy, TuitionStatus, HonorStudent)
HandicapAccommodation(AccommodationID)
HandicappedStudent(IDNumber, AccommodationID)
Noncitizen(IDNumber, OriginCountry)
Sport(SportID)
Athlete(IDNumber, SportID)
Department(DeptID, ChairIDNumber)
Program(ProgramID, DeptID)
Courses(ProgramID, CourseNumber, Credits)
PrereqSequel(PrereqProgram, PrereqCourse, SequelProgram, SequelCourse)
Classes(ProgramID, CourseNumber, SectionNumber, TeacherIDNumber, RoomID)
Classroom(RoomID, Capacity)
EnrolledIn(IDNumber, ProgramID, CourseNumber, SectionNumber)

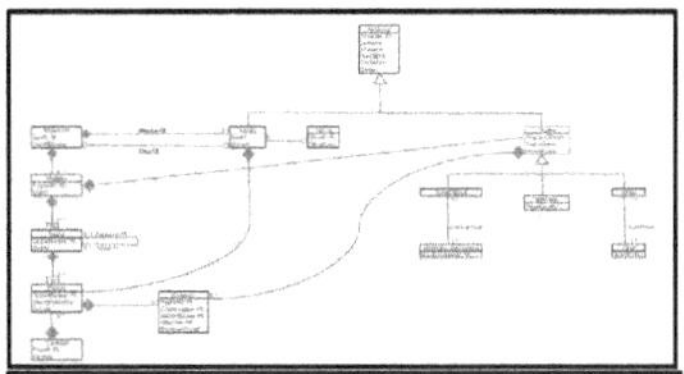

Figure 9-01

9.1.1 First Query

In our first query, we will ask about the relation "Classes"

We would like a list of all the sections of COMP1001 being offered.

Our query would go:

```
SELECT *
    FROM Classes
    WHERE ProgramID = 'COMP' AND CourseNumber = '1001' ;
```

This query illustrates the characteristic *select-from-where* form of most SQL queries.

The FROM clause identifies the relation(s) to which the query refers.

In our example, the query is about the tuples in relation Classes.

The WHERE clause is a condition. Tuples must satisfy this condition in order to match the query and be part of the query result.

In our example the condition is that the ProgramID attribute of the tuple have value 'COMP' and that the CourseNumber attribute have value '1001'. Most tuples in the "Classes" relation will probably fail one or the other (or both) of these conditions and will not be included in the resulting relation. Some of the tuples, however, will have both of these values for the attributes and, thus, satisfy the condition. These tuples will be included in the relation created by the query.

The SELECT clause controls which attributes will be included in the query result.

The symbol * as in our example, indicates that all of the attributes will be included in the output relation.

The query processor checks each tuple in the relation Classes. If, for example it encounters the tuple (COMP,1001,101,872104567,TU110) it will determine that the tuple does, indeed, satisfy the condition and will add the tuple to the list of tuples that will form the output relation.

ProgramID	CourseNumber	SectionNumber	TeacherIDNumber	RoomID
...	...	...	...	...
COMP	1001	011	824101234	TU212
COMP	1001	012	714034512	TU214
COMP	1001	101	872104567	TU110
COMP	1001	102	555122313	TU301
COMP	1001	113	897208366	AE103
...	...	...	...	...

Figure 9-02, at the right illustrates the kind of relation that would result from executing the example query.

Figure 9-02

9.1.2 Projection in SQL

As a general rule, we will not need all of the components/attributes of the tuples satisfying the condition(s) of a query and we can, if we wish, design a query which includes only the information needed.

We might want our query to *project* the relation from the complete query onto a subset of the attributes. In place of the * symbol in the SELECT clause, we would simply list the desired attributes of the relation(s) mentioned in the FROM clause.

All of the tuples produced by the above query would have the same values for attributes Program and Course, so it would not be necessary to include these values in the query result. We could, instead, execute the query:

SELECT **SectionNumber, TeacherIDNumber**
    FROM Classes
    WHERE ProgramID = 'COMP'
        AND CourseNumber = '1001' ;

SectionNumber	TeacherIDNumber
...	...
011	824101234
012	714034512
101	872104567
102	555122313
113	897208366
...	...

Figure 9-03

Executing this query might produce something like the relation shown in Figure 9-03.

9.1.3 Changing Column Headers

Sometimes we wish to produce a relation with attribute names (column headers) that are different from the attribute names of the original relation. We can achieve this effect using the keyword AS following the original name of the attribute.

The following query might produce something like the relation shown in Figure 9-04:

SELECT SectionNumber AS Section,
    TeacherIDNumber **AS FacID**
    FROM Classes
    WHERE ProgramID = 'COMP'
        AND CourseNumber = '1001' ;

Section	FacID
...	...
011	8241061234
012	7140354512
101	8721014567
102	5551212313
113	8972018366
...	...

Figure 9-04

9.2 Selection in SQL

The *selection* operator of relational algebra is available through the WHERE clause in SQL.

We can build expressions by comparing values using six common comparison operators:
$=, <>, <,>, <=, >=$

The values that can be compared include constants and values from attributes from the relation(s) of the FROM clause.

We can apply the usual arithmetic operators $(+,*,-,...)$ to numeric values to create new values for the comparisons.

We can apply the concatenation operator $\parallel$ to strings

Strings in SQL are denoted by surrounding sequences of characters with single quotes.

The results of comparisons are *boolean* values:

TRUE or FALSE.

Boolean values can be combined using logical operators AND, OR and NOT.

Recall our use of "AND" in our earlier example:
WHERE ProgramID = 'COMP' **AND** CourseNumber = '1001' ;

9.2.1 Comparison of Strings

Strings can be stored as either fixed length sequences or as variable length sequences

Fixed length strings are specified using CHAR( )

Variable length strings are specified using VARCHAR( )

When two strings with different declarations are compared for equality, only the *actual* strings are compared. Any extra "padding" characters that might have been appended to one of them will be ignored.

When comparing strings with operators $<$ or $>$, or $<=$ or $>=$, the lexicographic order is used.

String $a_1a_2...a_n$ is "less than" $b_1b_2...b_m$

if: $a_1 < b_1$

or if $a_1 = b_1$ and $a_2 < b_2$

or if $a_1 = b_1$ and $a_2 = b_2$ and $a_3 < b_3$

or if ...

Example:

SELECT *
FROM Classes
WHERE ProgramID = 'COMP'
AND CourseNumber = '1001'
AND SectionNumber >= '100' ;

ProgramID	CourseNumber	SectionNumber	TeacherIDNumber	RoomID
...	...	...		...
COMP	1001	101	872104567	TU110
COMP	1001	102	555122313	TU301
COMP	1001	113	897208366	AE103
...	...	...	...	...

Figure 9-05

9.2.2 Pattern Matching in SQL

SQL also provides the capability to compare strings on the basis of simple pattern matching. This pattern matching uses the format:

> s LIKE p

where s is a string and p is a *pattern*

> A *pattern* is a string which (may) include special characters % and _

> Ordinary characters in p match the same characters in s.

> The character % matches any sequence of 0 or more characters in s.

> The character _ in p matches any (single) character in s.

> Note that the representation of a string begins and ends with the single quote character '

> To represent a string which contains the single quote character, we must enter two copies of the character to indicate that we do not want the character to terminate the string.

Example: If we want a list of faculty members teaching in a classroom whose identifier contains a '0':

> SELECT TeacherIDNumber, RoomID
> FROM Classes
> WHERE **RoomID LIKE '%0%'** ;

TeacherIDNumber	RoomID
...	...
872104567	TU110
555122313	TU301
897208366	AE103
...	...

Figure 9-06

9.3 Dates and Times in SQL

Implementations of SQL usually support dates and times as special data types.

The SQL standard is very specific about date and time *storage* and data input formats, but in data output, dates and times can usually be *represented* in a variety of formats:

Examples:	05/14/1948	5/14/48	14 May 1948	May 14, 1948
	2:15 PM	14:15	14:15:00	

The date and time data types generally support *comparison* operations. The interpretation of these operations is as would be expected: "*less than*" means "*earlier than*"

9.3.1 SQL Format for DATE

A date is represented by the keyword DATE followed by a string of the form 'YYYY-MM-DD'

> A string consisting of four digits representing the year followed by a dash, followed by two digits representing the month followed by another dash followed by two digits representing the date.

Example: DATE '1948-05-14

Example:

> SELECT IDNumber
> FROM Personnel
> WHERE DateOfBirth >= DATE '1960-00-00';

IDNumber
...
824101234
714034512
872104567
555122313
897208366
...

Figure 9-07

9.3.2 SQL Format for TIME

A time constant is represented by the keyword TIME followed by a string of the form 'HH:MM:SS'

The string must have the form two digits (representing the hour - 24 hours per day) followed by a colon followed by two digits (representing a number of minutes) followed by another colon followed by two digits (representing a number of seconds.)

Example: TIME '14:24:00'

Fractions of seconds can be represented using decimals.

Example: TIME '15:30:00.5'

9.3.3 SQL Format for TIMESTAMP

We represent the combination of date and time with a value of type TIMESTAMP which combines formats of DATE and TIME

Example: TIMESTAMP '1948-05-14 12:30:00'

9.4 Null Values in SQL and Comparisons involving Null

SQL permits attributes to have a special value NULL, called the *null value*

There are several different ways a null value can be interpreted:

Value unknown

Value inapplicable

No possible value

Value withheld

We have seen that the use of the outerjoin operation can produce tuples with null values.

SQL supports the outerjoin operation, and, thus, must, of necessity, SQL must deal with tuples which have null values. SQL also supports other operations that can produce nulls.

In WHERE clauses, we must be prepared for situations where a component of some tuple we are examining might have a null value.

9.4.1 Rules for operating on NULL values

There are three important rules to remember when operating on NULL values.

When we operate on a NULL value using an arithmetic operator with any value (including another NULL) the result will be NULL

The result of the computation
   NULL – NULL
will be NULL (not 0)

When we compare a NULL value and any value (including NULL) using any of the comparison operators ($<, =, >$) the result will be UNKNOWN

The result of the comparison
   NULL = NULL
will be UNKNOWN (not TRUE)

The above rules apply to *expressions* whose value is NULL. We cannot use NULL explicitly as an operand.

If x is an expression with value NULL, then *x+3* has value NULL, however
    NULL+3
is an illegal SQL expression

The expression
    x = NULL
is not legal SQL, but NULL can be used with the operator IS and IS NOT.

The expression
    x IS NULL
is legal and will result in one of the values TRUE or FALSE, depending on whether the value of x is or is not NULL.

9.5 The Truth Value UNKNOWN

It is tempting to think of the result of any comparison as being either TRUE or FALSE, with no other alternatives, but
    (as we saw in 9.4.1 above)
the value resulting from a comparison can also be UNKNOWN.

We must, then, understand how the logical operators AND, OR and NOT operate in this
    (not so familiar)
three valued system.

If we think of TRUE as being 1, FALSE as 0 and UNKNOWN as ½, then we can interpret:

x AND y as MIN(x,y)

x OR y as MAX(x,y)

NOT x as 1-x

Truth table:				
x	y	x AND y	x OR y	NOT x
TRUE	TRUE	TRUE	TRUE	FALSE
TRUE	UNKNOWN	UNKNOWN	TRUE	FALSE
TRUE	FALSE	FALSE	TRUE	FALSE
UNKNOWN	TRUE	UNKNOWN	TRUE	UNKNOWN
UNKNOWN	UNKNOWN	UNKNOWN	UNKNOWN	UNKNOWN
UNKNOWN	FALSE	FALSE	UNKNOWN	UNKNOWN
FALSE	TRUE	FALSE	TRUE	TRUE
FALSE	UNKNOWN	FALSE	UNKNOWN	TRUE
FALSE	FALSE	FALSE	FALSE	TRUE

Figure 9-08

9.6 Ordering the Output

We often want the tuples in a query output to be presented in some sorted order. The order may be based on the value of some attribute, or list of attributes, in the same way that the values of projections can be ordered.

To construct an SQL query with this kind of *ordered* output, we can add an ORDER BY clause to the *SELECT-FROM-WHERE* sequence.

The ORDER BY clause has the form:

ORDER BY <list of attributes>

and is placed after all other clauses.

When an ORDER BY clause is used, tuples will, by default, be ordered in ascending order (least to greatest.)

We can, however, append the keyword DESC (for descending) to an attribute. (We can also add the keyword ASC, for ascending, but this is unnecessary, since this is the default behavior.)

If the order by list has more than one attribute, the result tuples will be ordered according the first attribute in the list. Tuples with identical values for the first attribute will be ordered according to their values in the second attribute in the list. Any tuples with identical values in the first two attributes will be ordered according to the third attribute, and so on.

The following query:

SELECT IDNumber, LastName, FirstName, Gender
FROM Personnel
ORDER BY Gender DESC, LastName, FirstName;

might produce a relation like that illustrated in Figure 9-09, with all tuples having "Gender" attribute 'M' coming before any having "Gender" 'F', all tuples with the same "Gender" attribute ordered (alphabetically) and those with identical "Gender" and "LastName" values ordered according to "FirstName".

IDNumber	LastName	FirstName	Gender
...	...	...	...
555122313	Branch	Arnold	M
555442523	Branch	Clifford	M
897208366	Wolf	Harry	M
...	...	...	...
824101234	Anderson	Julia	F
714034512	Sanders	Angela	F
872104567	Sanders	Barbara	F
...	...	...	...

Figure 9-09

9.7 Queries Involving More than One Relation

SQL has a simple way to reference data from multiple relations in one query.

Listing all of the relations in the FROM clause allows the SELECT and WHERE clauses to reference the attributes from any of the relations.

If a query references more than one relation, it is possible that two relations might have attributes with the same name. In such a case, it would be necessary to distinguish between the attributes (disambiguate them), so there must be a way to indicate which of the attributes is being referenced.

SQL solves this problem by allowing us to place the name of a relation followed by a dot in front of an attribute name[15]:

R.A would identify the attribute in relation R with attribute name A.

---

[15]   We can use this relation dot attribute notation even when there is no duplication of attribute names (no ambiguity.) In this situation the notation might serve a documentation function.

Example: Suppose we want to find the names of the teachers assigned to teach COMP1001. Note that the names of teachers are in relation "Personnel", but the attributes ProgramID and CourseNumber are in relation "Classes". A query, producing the desired information must reference attributes in both relations.

SELECT IDNumber, LastName, FirstName
  FROM Classes, Personnel
  WHERE ProgramID ='COMP' AND
      CourseNumber = '1001 AND
      Classes.TeacherIDNumber=Personnel.IDNumber;

IDNumber	LastName	FirstName
...	...	...
555122313	Branch	Arnold
555442523	Branch	Clifford
897208366	Wolf	Harry
824101234	Anderson	Julia
714034512	Sanders	Angela
872104567	Sanders	Barbara
...	...	...
	Figure 9-10	

9.7.1 Disambiguating Attributes

Disambiguating (i.e. distinguishing between multiple copies of) attributes using the relation name, as described above, works well as long as the attributes are in different relations, but sometimes we need to access different tuples from the same relation. For this kind of problem, we can list the same relation several times in the FROM clause, but, as we need a way to distinguish between the occurrences of the relation, we must assign an *alias* (also known as a tuple variable) to duplicate relations in the FROM statement. We assign the tuple variable using the [optional] keyword AS. Then we can use the tuple variable(s) the same way we would use relation name(s) in the "relation dot attribute" form.

Suppose we wanted a list of the pairs of teachers who share the same office.

SELECT First.IDNumber AS OfficeMate1, Second.IDNumber AS OfficeMate2,
      First.OfficeID AS Office
  FROM **Faculty As First, Faculty AS Second**
  WHERE **First**.OfficeID = **Second**.OfficeID
      AND **First**.IDNumber<**Second**.IDNumber;

OfficeMate1	OfficeMate2	Office
...	...	...
555122313	555442523	TU414
824101234	897208366	TU408
...	...	...
	Figure 9-11	

Note how we have used the condition
    First.IDNumber<Second.IDNumber
to avoid duplications in the results.

9.7.2 Interpreting Multirelation Queries

As we have just seen, the FROM clause in a query can involve more than one relation.

```
SELECT ...
FROM R1, R2, ... , Rn
WHERE ...
```

There are several (at least 3) different ways to interpret/define the meaning of the combinations of these multiple relations:

Nested Loops, *Parallel Assignment*, and *Cross Product*

These three interpretations are equivalent, at least in the sense that they all result in describing the same output.

9.7.2.1 Nested Loops

```
FOR each tuple t₁ in R1 DO
 FOR each tuple t₂ in R2 DO

  ...

  ...

   FOR each tuple tₙ in Rn DO
    IF (the collection t₁,t₂,...,tₙ satisfies the WHERE condition)
    THEN
     evaluate the SELECT clause for these values and add result to the output relation.
```

9.7.2.2 Parallel Assignment

```
FOREACH
    (tuple t₁ in R1, tuple t₂ in R2, ..., tuple tₙ in Rn)
DO
 IF (the combination t₁, t₂,...,tₙ satisfies the condition of the WHERE clause)
 THEN evaluate the SELECT clause for this combination and add result to output
relation
```

(Note that the only difference between parallel assignment and nested loops is the order in which the tuple combinations are processed.)

9.7.2.3 Cross Product

```
Calculate the product P=R1×R2×...×Rn
FOREACH p∈P DO
    IF (the attributes in p satisfy the WHERE condition)
    THEN
     evaluate the SELECT clause for the tuples in p and add the result to the output relation
```

The Database Language SQL

9.8 Union, Intersection and Difference of Queries

Sometimes we want to combine relations, using the standard set operations of union, intersection and difference.

SQL supports these operation, but only for collections of relations which have the same attribute names and data types.

– The keywords for these operations are UNION, INTERSECT and EXCEPT

– These keywords are placed between queries and the queries must be parenthesized.

(Note that these are *set* operations.)

Example with UNION:
Suppose we want to find the names of all women assigned to teach mathematics (ProgramID MATH) and/or computer (ProgramID COMP) courses.:

```
(SELECT LastName, FirstName
    FROM Personnel, Faculty, Classes
    WHERE Gender='F'
        AND ProgramID='COMP'
        AND TeacherIDNumber=Faculty.IDNumber
        AND Faculty.IDNumber=Personnel.IDNumber;)
UNION
(SELECT LastName, FirstName
    FROM Personnel, Faculty, Classes
    WHERE Gender='F'
        AND ProgramID='MATH'
        AND TeacherIDNumber=Faculty.IDNumber
        AND Faculty.IDNumber=Personnel.IDNumber;)
```

Example with INTERSECT:
Suppose we want a list of faculty offices assigned to both (at least one) woman and (at least one) man:

```
(SELECT OfficeID
    FROM Faculty, Personnel
    WHERE Gender = 'F'
        AND Personnel.IDNumber=Faculty.IDNumber;)
INTERSECT
(SELECT OfficeID
    FROM Faculty, Personnel
    WHERE Gender = 'M'
        AND Personnel.IDNumber=Faculty.IDNumber;)
```

Example with EXCEPT:

Suppose we want a list of all students who are not enrolled in any computer course:

```
(SELECT IDNumber
    FROM Student;)
EXCEPT
(SELECT IDNumber
    FROM EnrolledIn
    WHERE ProgramID = 'COMP;')
```

Note that in all of these examples, the relations (conveniently) had attributes with the same names (and the same data types.) If necessary, we can rename attributes to achieve this effect.

```
SELECT a AS b, c AS d, …
```

9.9 Subqueries in SQL

In SQL, queries can be used (in various ways) to help in the evaluation of other queries.

A query that is part of (included within) another is called a *subquery*. (Subqueries, by the way, can also contain subqueries.)

There are a number of ways that subqueries can be used.

9.9.1 Subqueries Returning Single Constants

A subquery can return a single constant and this constant can be compared with another value in a WHERE clause.

A value that can appear as one component of a tuple is referred to as a *scalar*.

A *select-from-where* expression can produce a relation with any number of attributes and any number of tuples, but we are often interested in only one attribute and can deduce that there will be only one value produced for that attribute.

In such a case, we can use such a "*select-from-where*" subquery (surrounded by parentheses) as if it were a constant.

A relation returned by a subquery can be used in either a WHERE clause or in a FROM clause;

```
SELECT IDNumber, ProgramID, CourseNumber, SectionNumber
    FROM EnrolledIn
    WHERE ProgramID = 'COMP'
        AND 'F'=
            ( SELECT Gender
            FROM EnrolledIn, Student
            WHERE EnrolledIn.IDNumber=Student.IDNumber; );
```

9.9.2 Subqueries Returning Relations

A *select-from-where* expression can produce a relation with any number of attributes and any number of tuples.

Such an expression can be used where a relation with a similar collection of attributes could be used.

Example: If we wanted a list of office telephone numbers of professors teaching mathematics courses, we might use

```
SELECT MathID, OfficePhone
    FROM Offices, Faculty,
        (SELECT Faculty.IDNumber AS MathID
         FROM Faculty, Classes
         WHERE Faculty.IDNumber=Classes.TeacherIDNumber
            AND Classes.ProgramID='MATH';)
        WHERE Offices.OfficeID=Faculty.OfficeID AND Faculty.IDNumber=MathID;
```

9.9.3 SQL Conditions Involving Relations

There are four SQL operations that we can apply to a relation R and obtain a boolean value as a result. These four operators are:
- EXISTS
- IN
- ALL
- ANY

These operations apply only to relations created by subqueries. It would be common to see the argument of one of the operators to have the form (SELECT * FROM R)

9.9.3.1 The EXISTS operation

EXISTS R is a condition that will be true if and only if the relation R is nonempty (and, of course, false if R *is* empty.)

The operator EXISTS can be negated by putting NOT in front of the expression

NOT EXISTS R will be true if and only if R is empty.

Example:

To find any offices with no teachers assigned to them:

```
SELECT OfficeID
FROM Offices
WHERE NOT EXISTS (
    SELECT *
    FROM Faculty
    WHERE Offices.OfficeID = Faculty.OfficeID
    );
```

9.9.3.2 The IN operation

Assuming, for the moment, that R is a unary relation and s is a scalar[16],

The operation
> s IN R

will be true if and only if s is equal to one of the values in R

Likewise
> s NOT IN R

will be false if s *is* equal to one of the values in R.

Example:

To find any classrooms with no classes meeting in them:

```
SELECT RoomID
FROM Classroom
WHERE RoomID NOT IN (
    SELECT RoomID
    FROM Classes
);
```

9.9.3.3 The ALL operation

The ALL operation will be used in combination with a comparison operator and a subquery which produces a relation R. The combination will result in value *true* if the comparison operation results in *true* for each value in R.

Again, we assume that R is a unary relation produced by a subquery and s is a scalar.

The operation
> s > ALL R

will be true if and only if s is greater than every value in R.
> NOT s > ALL R

will be true if there is some value in R greater than or equal to s.

The relation > can be replaced by any of the other five comparison operators.

9.9.3.4 The ANY operation

The ANY operation will be used in combination with a comparison operator and a subquery which produces a relation R. The combination will result in value *true* if the comparison operation results in *true* for at least one value in R.

Once again, we assume that R is a unary relation and s is a scalar.

The operation
> s > ANY R

will be true if and only if s is greater than *some* value in R.
> NOT s > ANY R

will be true if every value in R is greater than or equal to s.

The relation > can be replaced by any of the other five comparison operators.

---

[16] (We will deal later with the case where R has more than one attribute and s is a tuple)

9.9.4 SQL Conditions Involving Tuples

If a tuple t has the same number of components as a relation R has attributes (and if the corresponding attributes have compatible data types), then it makes sense to compare t with tuples in R, using the condition operators of the previous sections.

Most queries involving nested subqueries can be written as a single *select-from-where* query, but it is often the case that queries with nested subqueries will execute faster than the simpler *select-from-where* version.

9.9.4.1 Correlated Subqueries

In the simplest cases, a subquery can be evaluated once and the results used in all other parts of the containing query.

A more complex use of nested subqueries, however, will involve subqueries that must be evaluated many times, once for each assignment of a value to some term of the subquery.

A subquery of this type is called a *correlated* subquery.

In writing/analyzing correlated subqueries, it is important to be aware of the scoping rules for names.

An attribute in a subquery will normally belong to one of the tuple variables in the FROM clause of the subquery.

If the attribute is not included in the subquery's FROM clause, then it will be identified with an attribute in the FROM clause of the query which contains the subquery.

If there is no match, and the containing query is itself a subquery, then the attribute will be checked against the attributes in the FROM clause of the next containing query,

… and so on until a matching attribute is found

We can arrange that an attribute belong to another tuple variable by prefixing the reference by the tuple variable and a dot.

In a FROM list, we may insert a parenthesized subquery. Since the result relation of the subquery would not have a name, we would have to assign one using an alias.

9.10 SQL Join Operations

We can construct a relation using any of several variations of the join operator: products, natural joins, theta joins and outerjoins.

Each of these produces a relation and can be used as either a query or a subquery.

9.10.1 CROSS JOIN

The simplest form of join is the Cartesian product (or just *product*.)

The SQL expression that will create this kind of join is CROSS JOIN.

The expression

Faculty CROSS JOIN Offices

will produce a 5 column relation, one column for each attribute in each of the relations "Faculty" and "Offices".

IDNumber	DeptID	Faculty.OfficeID	Offices.OfficeID	OfficePhone

The relation described/produced by this expression will include every combination of a tuple from "Faculty" and a tuple from "Offices" (the Cartesian product.)

9.10.2 THETA JOIN

The CROSS JOIN operation is seldom very useful. A much more useful (and more common) operation is the *theta join*, which, in SQL, we specify with the keyword JOIN between the relation names, and the keyword ON which identifies the (theta) condition.

Example: The expression

Faculty JOIN Offices ON Faculty.OfficeID=Offices.OfficeID

will produce a relation with the same 5 attributes as the CROSS JOIN, one column for each attribute in each of the relations "Faculty" and "Offices" This "THETA JOIN" produces a relation in which the tuple combination satisfies the condition that every tuple in the join relation has the same values in the Faculty.OfficeID and Offices.OfficeID attributes.

9.10.3 NATURAL JOIN

The information in the example of 9.10.2 could have been obtained using a NATURAL JOIN, rather than the theta join.

A *natural join* is similar to a theta join, but differs in that for a natural join, the join condition must be that all pairs of attributes with common names are equated, and there are no other conditions (as was the case in 9.10.2).

Each pair of equated attributes will be represented by only one copy in the output tuple.

The SQL expression for this operation is "NATURAL JOIN".

The expression

Faculty NATURAL JOIN Offices

Would produce a relation with attributes:

IDNumber	DeptID	OfficeID	OfficePhone

The expression

Classes NATURAL JOIN EnrolledIn

Would produce a relation with attributes:

ProgramID	CourseNumber	SectionNumber	TeacherIDNumber	RoomID	IDNumber

9.10.4 SQL Outerjoins

In the "Faculty" join "Office" examples from 9.10.2 and 9.10.3 above, a professor who has not been assigned an office would not be represented in the resulting relation. Neither would an office with no faculty members assigned. The *outer join* operations support the creation of relations that include the information from such *dangling* tuples.

Recall that an outerjoin augments the result of a join by padding the contents of dangling tuple with null values.

SQL refers to the standard outerjoin (which pads dangling tuples from both relations) as a "*full outerjoin*".

a FULL OUTER JOIN b

a NATURAL FULL OUTER JOIN b

SQL also has operations for *left outerjoin*'s and *right outerjoin*'s.

All of the variations of outerjoins are available in SQL.

For a *theta* outerjoin rather than a natural outerjoin in SQL, we simply eliminate the keyword NATURAL and insert the keyword ON followed by the appropriate condition.

Examples:

The expression

    Classes LEFT OUTER JOIN Faculty ON TeacherIDNumber = IDNumber

produces a relation with all classes represented. A tuple in which the "Class" attributes identify a class which has been assigned a teacher will include the information for that teacher, but a tuple for a class with no teacher will have NULL's in the Faculty attributes.

The college might (almost certainly does) have courses that are not currently being offered. The query:

    SELECT *
    FROM Courses NATURAL LEFT OUTER JOIN Classes;

produces a relation with attributes

ProgramID	CourseNumber	Credits	SectionNumber	TeacherIDNumber
...	...	...	...	...

Every tuple in the relation "Courses" will be represented in the join (multiple times if more than one section of the course is currently being offered) If a course is not being offered, a tuple with its "ProgramID", "CourseNumber" and "Credits" attribute values will be included, and assigned NULL values for the "SectionNumber" and "TeacherIDNumber" attributes.

There might be professors who have not been assigned offices and there might also be offices that have not been assigned to professors.

The query:

    SELECT *
    FROM Faculty NATURAL FULL OUTER JOIN Offices;

will result in a relation with attributes as in 9.10.3. Each faculty member will appear in (at least) one tuple and each office will appear in (at least one) tuple. A tuple identifying a faculty member with no office will have NULL in OfficeID and OfficePhone. A tuple identifying an office with nobody assigned will have NULL's for the Faculty attributes.

9.11 SQL Relation Operations

SQL provides operations for converting bags to sets, for converting sets to bags, for grouping and for aggregating.

Most SQL operations produce relations that are *bags* rather than *sets:*

(A tuple can appear more than once in the same relation.)

It is, however, possible to *force* the result of an operation to be a set rather than a bag.

(Using the keyword "DISTINCT")

There are, however, *some* operations that do produce *sets* by default, and sometimes we will prefer the *bag* form of the result, rather than the *set* form.

9.11.1 Eliminating Duplicates

When a(n) SQL query generates a new relation, it does not ordinarily eliminate duplicates.

(as we said earlier, by default queries produce bags rather than sets.)

If we do not want duplicate tuples in the result of a query, we may follow the SELECT keyword by the keyword DISTINCT.

Example:

```
SELECT DISTINCT TeacherID
FROM Classes
WHERE ProgramID = 'COMP';
```

9.11.2 Duplicates in Unions Intersections and Differences

Unlike the SELECT operator, the set operations UNION, INTERSECT and EXCEPT normally *eliminate* duplicates.

Bags are converted to sets and the operation is applied to the sets.

In order to prevent the elimination of duplicates, we must follow the operator keyword by the keyword ALL

Example: If there are multiple students/faculty with the same names, the UNION example query of 9.8 will produce only one tuple with a given LastName, FirstName combination. If we want each teacher/student name listed as many times as the name is used, we might execute the query:

```
(SELECT LastName, FirstName
    FROM Personnel, Faculty, Classes
    WHERE Gender='F'
        AND ProgramID='COMP'
        AND TeacherIDNumber=Faculty.IDNumber
        AND Faculty.IDNumber=Personnel.IDNumber;)
UNION ALL
((SELECT LastName, FirstName
    FROM Personnel, Faculty, Classes
    WHERE Gender='F'
        AND ProgramID='MATH'
        AND TeacherIDNumber=Faculty.IDNumber
        AND Faculty.IDNumber=Personnel.IDNumber;)
```

SQL also provides *bag* operators INTERSECT ALL and EXCEPT ALL.

If a tuple appears m times in R and n times in S, then in the relation produced by
    R INTERSECT ALL S
it will appear $MIN(m,n)$ times.

If a tuple appears m times in R and n times in S, then in the relation produced by
    R EXCEPT ALL S
it will appear $MAX(0, m-n)$ times.

9.11.3 Grouping and Aggregation in SQL

SQL provides the aggregation operators SUM, AVG, MIN, MAX and COUNT. These operators are used by applying them to a scalar valued expression (typically a column name) in a SELECT clause.

(An exception is the expression COUNT(*) which returns the number of *tuples* in a relation.)

The following query:

SELECT SUM(Credits), COUNT(Classes), COUNT(DISTINCT TeacherIDNumber)
FROM Classes;

returns:

the sum of the values in the Credits attributes of the tuples in relation Classes,

the number of tuples in the relation Classes

and the number of distinct values in the TeacherIDNumber attributes in relation Classes.

Recall (from 8.2.3) that, in relational algebra, the grouping-and-aggregation operator γ allows us to partition tuples in a relation into groups based on values of the tuples, and then apply aggregation operators to other columns, doing the aggregation separately for each of the different groups.

SQL provides a GROUP BY clause to support this capability, the grouping of the tuples of a relation. The GROUP BY clause follows the WHERE clause.

The keywords GROUP BY would be followed by a list of grouping attributes.

We also have the option of eliminating duplicates (using the keyword DISTINCT) before applying an aggregation operator.

Any aggregation operators are used in the SELECT clause are applied only within the groups.

Examples:

SELECT TeacherIDNumber, SUM(Credits)
FROM Classes
GROUP BY TeacherIDNumber;

SELECT ProgramID, CourseNumber, SectionNumber, COUNT(IDNumber)
FROM EnrolledIn
GROUP BY ProgramID, CourseNumber, SectionNumber;

Note that in these queries, the SELECT clauses have only two kinds of terms:

Attributes that appear in the GROUP BY clause

Aggregation terms: (an aggregation operator applied to an attribute or expression involving attributes.)

These are the only kind of terms that are allowed to appear in any SELECT clause that includes an aggregated term.

9.11.4 Grouping, Aggregation, and Nulls in SQL

When tuples have nulls, there are a few rules we must remember:

- The value NULL is ignored in any aggregation.

  - It does not contribute to a sum, average or count of an attribute

- COUNT(*) will always return the number of tuples in a relation, but COUNT(A) will return the number of *non-null* values of attribute A in the relation.

  - NULL however, is treated as an ordinary value when forming groups.

- We can have a group in which one or more of the grouping attributes is assigned the value NULL.

  - When any aggregation operation, except COUNT, is applied to an empty bag, the result will be NULL. The count of an empty bag is 0.

9.11.5 HAVING Clauses in SQL

Sometimes we will want to restrict our queries in ways that would require conditions based on aggregate properties. To do this we can use the HAVING keyword.

The HAVING clause was added to SQL because the WHERE keyword could not be used with aggregate functions.

- a *HAVING* clause must follow the GROUP BY clause

  - a *HAVING* clause consists of the keyword HAVING followed by a condition that can be applied to tuples in groups created by the GROUP BY clause.

- Any attribute of any relation in the FROM clause can be aggregated in the HAVING clause but only attributes that appear in the GROUP BY clause can appear unaggregated in the HAVING clause

Example:

```
SELECT ProgramID, CourseNumber, SectionNumber, COUNT(IDNumber)
FROM EnrolledIn
GROUP BY ProgramID, CourseNumber, SectionNumber
HAVING COUNT(IDNumber)<20;
```

9.12 SQL Database Modifications

Up to now we have focused on normal SQL *query* forms, and, in particular, statements using the *select-from-where* format.

There are, however, a number of other SQL statement forms, statements that do not return a result, but instead, change the state of the database.

We refer to these types of operations as *modifications*.

Among these are statements that allow us to:

Insert tuples into a relation

Delete certain tuples from a relation

Update values of some of the components of some of the existing tuples

9.12.1 Insertions

The basic form of the insertion statement is:

INSERT INTO R(A1,,,An) VALUES (v1,,,vn)

where R is a relation, Ai is an attribute of R and vi is the value to be inserted into attribute Ai

When the INSERT INTO operation is executed, a new tuple is created in relation R. The attributes Ai of relation R will be assigned the values vi.

If R has attributes that are not in the list, they will be assigned default values (Often NULL).

Example:

INSERT INTO
    Personnel(IDNumber,LastName,FirstName,SocSecNum,Gender)
VALUES
    ('702238765', 'Rabbit', 'Jack', '454123321', 'M');

If, as in the next example, we provide values for all attributes of the relation (in the proper order) it is not necessary to list the attribute names in the INSERT INTO command:

Example:

INSERT INTO EnrolledIn
VALUES('7023459753', 'COMP', '1001', '113');

Each of the INSERT's described above will place only a single tuple into the relation.

Rather than using explicit values for one tuple, it will often be more convenient to use a subquery to compute the values for a *set* of tuples to be inserted.

9.12.2 Deletions

The form of a deletion statement is:

DELETE FROM *R* WHERE <condition>

The result of executing this command is to remove all tuples satisfying the condition from relation *R*.

Example:

DELETE FROM EnrolledIn
WHERE ProgramID='COMP'
    AND CourseNumber = '1001'
    AND SectionNumber = '143';

9.12.3 Updates

To change the value of an attribute in an existing tuple, we use the UPDATE operator.

The general form of the UPDATE operator is:

UPDATE *R* SET <*new-value assignments*> WHERE <condition>

with *new-value assignments* being one or more statements of the form
    attribute, equal sign, expression

Example:

UPDATE Classes SET TeacherIDNumber=NULL
WHERE ProgramID='COMP'
    AND CourseNumber='1001'
    AND SectionNumber='101';

9.13 SQL Transactions

Up to now we have been assuming that:

Database operations are executed one at a time

The database state left by one operation is the state on which the next operation acts

Operations are carried out in their entirety ("atomically" – no hardware or software failures in the middle of an operation)

Real life is much more complicated than this.

In many applications (Web services, banking, airline reservations, ...) many users might be accessing the same database at the same time. This kind of situation could result in serious data errors.

Example: In an airline reservation system, it is entirely possible that two users might access the same flight at the same time. This could lead to the following kind of sequence:

User1 displays the available seats on the flight and sees that seat 12B is available.

User2 displays the available seats on the flight and sees that seat 12B is available.

User1 selects seat 12B

User2 selects seat 12B

Now both users believe they have reserved seat 12B.

9.13.1 Serializability

SQL allows the programmer to avoid the type of error illustrated in the above example by grouping several operations into one *transaction* and declaring that the transaction be *serializable* with respect to other transactions

Declaring a transaction as serializable establishes that there can be no overlap with other transactions. Once the system begins executing this transaction, no other transaction can begin executing until this one has finished.

9.13.2 Atomicity

It is possible for a single operation to put a database in an unacceptable state if there is a "crash" while the operation is running.

As an example, suppose a bank has a database, and one of the relations in that database is

Accounts(acctNo, balance)

Transferring $100 from one account (account 1755) to another (account 1756) requires two queries, something like:

UPDATE Accounts SET balance = balance + 100 WHERE acctNo = 1756;

UPDATE Accounts SET balance = balance – 100 WHERE acctNo = 1755;

If one of these queries were to be executed, and then for some reason the second were to fail to execute, then the bank's database would be left in an incorrect state. Either $100 would have appeared in account 1756 out of nowhere, or $100 would have simply disappeared from account 1755.

This example shows that certain combinations of operations must be done *atomically* – either all or none.

9.13.3 Transactions

The solution to serialization and atomicity is to group operations into *transactions*.

A *transaction* is a collection of one or more operations on the database that must be executed atomically: either all of the operations are performed (successfully) or none are performed.

In addition, SQL requires (by default) that the operations in a transaction be executed in a serializable manner.

The SQL command START TRANSACTION is used to mark the beginning of a transaction. There are two ways to *end* a transaction:

- Executing the SQL statement COMMIT

    causes the transaction to end successfully. Changes made since the initiation of the transaction are installed permanently to database.

- Executing the SQL Statement ROLLBACK

    causes the transaction to abort. Changes made since beginning of the transaction are undone (rolled back) not installed in the database.

9.13.4 SQL Read-Only Transactions

Initiating a transaction has the effect of blocking other users and this slows the system performance.

Many database accesses involve the reading data from the database and then, possibly, (depending on what was read) writing something to the database. This type of interaction is prone to serialization problems. Other transactions should be blocked from access to any data that might be modified by the write process.

There are, however, transactions that will *not* write to/modify the database (such transactions are called *read-only* transactions.) If a transaction will make no changes to the database (will not write to the database) then the system can take advantage of this fact. Other transactions (at least other read-only transactions) can also safely access the data simultaneously. Identifying a transaction as being a *read-only* transaction will have the effect of permitting other transactions to proceed, and thus improving system performance.

We tell the SQL system that the next transaction will be read-only by:

    SET TRANSACTION READ ONLY;

This statement must be executed before the transaction begins.

It is also legal to write:

    SET TRANSACTION READ WRITE;

but this is the default status.

9.13.5 Dirty Reads

Dirty data is a common term used to describe data that has been written by a transaction that has not yet been committed. A *dirty read* is a read of dirty data written by another transaction.

The risk of reading dirty data is that the transaction doing the writing may eventually abort. In this case, the dirty data would be removed from the database and the system is supposed to proceed as if the transaction had never happened. Sometimes the consequences of a dirty read might be serious and should be avoided. Sometimes the consequences would be relatively minor and it would make sense to allow them, in interest of faster execution.

Allowing dirty reads avoids:

Extra processing necessary to avoid the dirty reads (which takes extra time.)

Loss of parallelism that results from waiting until there is no possibility of a dirty read (until the transaction finishes.)

SQL allows us to specify that dirty reads are acceptable for a specific transaction. The appropriate form to establish such a transaction would be:

ISOLATION LEVEL READ UNCOMMITTED;

This isolation level sets default of READ-ONLY.

If we want the transaction to be able to modify data in the database, we must use the form:

SET TRANSACTION READ WRITE ISOLATION LEVEL READ UNCOMMITTED;

9.13.6 Isolation Levels

SQL has a total of four isolation levels:

– Serializable

No dirty reads, does not allow writes by other transactions.

– Read-uncommitted

Reads data from database, whether committed or uncommitted.

– Read-committed

Reads only committed data from database. Other transactions can run in parallel and modify data. The read-committed transaction will not read dirty data but, if the query runs multiple times, it might get different values.

– Repeatable-read

Reads only committed data. If a query reads a tuple in one execution, it will read the same tuple when executed again, but the second execution would read any tuples inserted after the first execution (phantom tuples)

The Database Language SQL

9.14 Chapter 9 Questions

9.14.1 True-False

9.14.1.1 There are many different dialects of SQL.

9.14.1.2 Strings in SQL are denoted by surrounding them by either single quotes or double quotes.

9.14.1.3 Strings in SQL are denoted by surrounding them by either single quotes or double quotes.

9.14.1 4 Strings in SQL are stored as fixed length sequences.

9.14.1.5 Strings in SQL can be stored as either fixed length sequences or as variable length sequences.

9.14.1.6 The operation s IN R will be *true* if and only if s is equal to one of the values in R
  • Likewise s NOT IN R will be *false* if s is equal to one of the values in R.

9.14.1.7 The query:
SELECT * FROM *Courses NATURAL LEFT OUTER JOIN Classes;*
produces a relation in which every tuple from relation Classes appears in at least one tuple. If the tuple does not match any tuple from Courses, then the Courses attributes that do not appear in Classes will have null values.

9.14.1.8 SQL requires (by default) that the operations in a transaction be executed atomically and in a serializable manner.

9.14.2 Multiple Choice

9.14.2.1 Most *SQL queries use the keyword* _____
  a. SELECT
  b. FROM
  c. WHERE
  d. all of the above
  e. none of the above

9.14.2.2 When we operate on a NULL value using a comparison operator with any value (including another NULL) the result will be _____
  a. NULL
  b. UNKNOWN
  c. 0
  d. FALSE
  e. none of the above

9.14.2.3 The operator _____ normally eliminates duplicates
  a. UNION
  b. INTERSECT
  c. EXCEPT
  d. all of the above
  e. none of the above

9.14.2.4 A *HAVING* clause must follow the _____ clause
  a. SELECT
  b. FROM
  c. WHERE
  d. any of the above
  e. none of the above

9.14.3 Completion

9.14.3.1 The most commonly used relational DBMS's use a language called _____ to query and modify the databases.

9.14.3.2 SQL serves both as a data manipulation language and as a data _____ language.

9.14.3.3 In an SQL query, the _____ clause is a condition. Tuples must satisfy this condition in order to match the query and be part of the query result.

9.14.3.4 In an SQL query, the symbol _____ in the SELECT clause indicates that the entire tuple is produced in the result.

9.14.3.5 Sometimes we wish to produce a relation with column headers different from the attribute names from the original relation.
  • We can achieve this effect using the keyword _____ following the original name of the attribute.

9.14.3.6 A pattern in SQL is a string which (may) include special characters _____ and _

9.14.3.7 SQL provides the capability to compare strings on the basis of simple pattern matching.
  – Using the form :
      s LIKE p
  where s is a string and p is a *pattern*
  • Ordinary characters in p match the same characters in s.
    The character _____ matches any sequence of 0 or more characters in s

9.14.3.8 In official SQL, a date is represented by the keyword _____ followed by a string of the form 'YYYY-MM-DD'

9.14.3.9 We can assign a(n) _____ (also known as a *tuple variable*) to any relation in the FROM statement.

9.14.3.10 Sometimes we want to combine relations, using the standard set operations of union, intersection and difference.
  SQL allows us to do this, with relations having the same attribute names and data types.
  – The keywords are UNION, INTERSECT and _____

9.14.3.11 A value that can appear as one component of a tuple is referred to as a(n) _____

9.14.3.12 There are a number of SQL operations that we can apply to a relation R and obtain a boolean result.
The operators are:
- EXISTS
- _____
- ALL
- ANY

9.14.3.13 _____ R is a condition that will be true if and only if R is nonempty.

9.14.3.14 The INTERSECT ALL and EXCEPT ALL operators are _____ operators.

9.14.3.15 To change the value of an attribute in a tuple that already exists, we use the SQL _____ operator.

9.14.3.16 The solution to problems of serialization and atomicity is to group operations into _____

9.14.3.17 The SQL statement _____ causes the transaction to end successfully. Changes made since transaction began are installed permanently to database.

9.14.3.18 _____ *data* is a common term for data written by a transaction that has not yet been committed.

Constraints

10.0 Constraints

SQL provides a variety of techniques for expressing integrity constraints as part of a database schema.

We have already seen one kind of constraint: key constraints.

The requirement that an attribute or set of attributes be a key for a relation.

SQL also supports a form of *referential* integrity called *foreign key constraint*

The requirement that a value for an attribute or set of attributes of a relation must also appear as value in another relation

SQL also provides support for constraints on attributes, constraints on tuples and interrelation constraints called *assertions*.

10.1 Keys and Foreign Keys

SQL allows us to specify that an attribute or a collection of attributes is a key for a relation by using the keywords PRIMARY KEY or the keyword UNIQUE.

SQL also uses the term "key" in relation to certain *referential integrity* constraints. These constraints, called "foreign key constraints", assert that a value appearing in one relation must also appear (as primary key value) in another relation.

10.1.1 Declaring Foreign Key Constraints

A *foreign key* constraint is an assertion that values for certain attributes must have appropriate values, values that appear in specific attributes in other relations.

In the "Classes" relation, the "TeacherIDNumber" attribute is supposed to identify the teacher assigned to teach the class. Its value should be the same as a value in the "IDNumber" attribute in a tuple in the "Faculty" relation.

In SQL, we may declare an attribute or attributes of a relation to be a foreign key referencing some (probably other) relation. This has two consequences:

The referenced attributes of the second relation must be declared as either UNIQUE or as PRIMARY KEY.

The foreign key declaration imposes the requirement that values of the foreign key attribute(s) must appear as the values of the referenced attribute(s) in tuples of the referenced relation.

In the CREATE TABLE statement a foreign key can be declared in either of two ways:

- If the foreign key is a single attribute, we may follow the name and type by a declaration that it "references" some attribute (which must be a key) of some table.
  <name> <type> REFERENCES <table> (<attribute name>)

- Alternatively, we may append to the list of attributes a declaration stating that a set of attributes is a foreign key, then giving the table name and the attribute(s) referenced (which must be a key)
  FOREIGN KEY (<attribute(s)>) REFERENCES <table> (<attribute(s)>)

Constraints

Example:

```
CREATE TABLE Classes(
    ProgramID CHAR(4),
    CourseNumber CHAR(4),
    SectionNumber CHAR(3),
    TeacherIDNumber CHAR(9)
        FOREIGN KEY REFERENCES Faculty (IDNumber),
    RoomID CHAR(5)
        FOREIGN KEY REFERENCES Classroom(RoomID),
    PRIMARY KEY (ProgramID, CourseNumber, SectionNumber),
    FOREIGN KEY (ProgramID, CourseNumber)
        REFERENCES Courses(ProgramID, CourseNumber)
);
```

10.1.2 Declaring Foreign Key Constraints

There are two kinds of errors that a foreign key declaration prevents:

Modifications of the table *with* the foreign key declaration which will either:

Attempt to insert a tuple with a (nonnull) value for the foreign key attribute(s) which does not match any value in the referenced attribute(s).

Attempt to update a tuple, placing a (nonnull) value in the foreign key attribute(s) which does not match any value in the referenced attribute(s).

Either of these will generate a run time error.

Modifications of the referenced table, resulting in:

Deletion of a tuple with value in the referenced attribute(s) which matches one or more of the foreign key values.

Update of a tuple which changes a value in the referenced attribute(s) which matches one or more of the foreign key values of one or more tuples in the referencing table.

The database designer can choose among three different ways to deal with modifications of referenced tables.

10.1.2.1 Rejecting Changes

The default policy is to simply reject any change that would result in a violation of a referential integrity constraint. Attempts to do so will generate error messages.

10.1.2.2 Cascade policy

Under this policy, changes in the referenced attribute(s) are mimicked in the relations referencing the changed attribute(s).

10.1.2.3 Set NULL Policy

When a change in a referenced relation affects a foreign key value, the value(s) of the referencing tuple attribute(s) is/are set to NULL.

10.1.3 Deletes and/or Updates

The above options are chosen for deletes and for updates separately and are programmed in the declaration of the foreign key.

Example:

```
CREATE TABLE Faculty(
    IDNumber CHAR(9) PRIMARY KEY,
    Office CHAR(6) FOREIGN KEY
        REFERENCES Offices(OfficeID)
        ON DELETE SET NULL
        ON UPDATE CASCADE,
    DeptID CHAR(4) FOREIGN KEY
        REFERENCES Department(DeptID)
        ON DELETE SET NULL
        ON UPDATE CASCADE,
    Gender CHAR(1)
);
```

10.1.4 Deferred Checking of Constraints

Sometimes a database schema might involve circular constraints, making it impossible to modify either relation without modifying the other first. Consider the following example[17]:

```
CREATE TABLE Department(
    DeptID VARCHAR(20) PRIMARY KEY,
    DepartmentChair CHAR(9)
        NOT NULL
        FOREIGN KEY
            REFERENCES DeptChairList (ChairID)
            ON UPDATE CASCADE,
    DeptOffice CHAR(6)
        FOREIGN KEY
            REFERENCES Offices(OfficeID)
            ON DELETE SET NULL
            ON UPDATE CASCADE,
);

CREATE TABLE DeptChairList(
    ChairID CHAR(9) PRIMARY KEY
        FOREIGN KEY REFERENCES Faculty(IDNumber)
        ON UPDATE CASCADE,
    Dept VARCHAR(20) UNIQUE
        FOREIGN KEY
        REFERENCES Department(DeptID)
);
```

---

[17] Not an example of a structure we recommend emulating.

Constraints

With this database design, the addition of a new department requires an entry in the DeptChairList, but a tuple in the table DeptChairList must have a value for its DeptID attribute. No tuple of either relation could be entered, because it would have to reference a tuple that would first have to have been entered in the other.

To support this kind of structure, SQL provides the option:
> DEFERRABLE INITIALLY DEFERRED

option that can be added to the declaration of a constraint.

A DEFERRABLE INITIALLY DEFERRED constraint will not be checked immediately, but instead it will be checked at the end of the transaction that contains it.

Example:

```
CREATE TABLE Department(
    DeptID VARCHAR(20) PRIMARY KEY,
    DepartmentChair CHAR(9)
        NOT NULL
        FOREIGN KEY
            REFERENCES DeptChairList (ChairID)
            ON UPDATE CASCADE
            DEFERRABLE INITIALLY DEFERRED,
    DeptOffice CHAR(6)
        FOREIGN KEY
            REFERENCES Offices(OfficeID)
            ON DELETE SET NULL
            ON UPDATE CASCADE,
);
CREATE TABLE DeptChairList(
    ChairID CHAR(9) PRIMARY KEY
        FOREIGN KEY REFERENCES Faculty(IDNumber)
        ON UPDATE CASCADE,
    Dept VARCHAR(20) UNIQUE
        FOREIGN KEY
        REFERENCES Department(DeptID)
        DEFERRABLE INITIALLY DEFERRED
);
```

With these schemas, the process of adding a new department would require a sequence something like the following:

```
START Transaction
    INSERT INTO Department(DeptID, DepartmentChair, DeptOffice)
    Values('PseudoParaPsychology','242236666', 'OFF313')
    INSERT INTO DeptChairList(ChairID, Dept)
    VALUES('242236666', 'PseudoParaPsychology')
COMMIT;
```

With this process the department name foreign key constraints will not be checked until after both tuples have been entered.

Constraints

10.2 Constraints on Attributes and Tuples

In a(n) SQL CREATE TABLE statement, we can declare two kinds of constraints: constraints on individual attributes and constraints on tuples as a whole.

10.2.1 Single Attribute Constraint: NOT NULL

A simple constraint to define for an attribute is that it be NOT NULL. This constraint has the effect of disallowing any tuple in which the value for this attribute is NULL.

The constraint is declared by the keywords NOT NULL following the declaration of the attribute in the CREATE TABLE statement

(For an example, see

```
DepartmentChair CHAR(9)
    NOT NULL
```

In the "Department" table declaration in section 10.1.2.5 above.)

10.2.2 Single Attribute CHECK Constraint

Constraints can also be attached to attributes by the keyword CHECK and a parenthesized condition that must hold for every value of that attribute.

Example:

```
CREATE TABLE Personnel(
    IDNumber CHAR(9) PRIMARY KEY,
    SocSecNum CHAR(9) UNIQUE,
    LastName VARCHAR(25),
    FirstName VARCHAR(25),
    Gender CHAR(1) CHECK (Gender IN ('M', 'F'))
);
```

10.2.3 Tuple Based CHECK Constraints

To declare a constraint on *tuples* of a single relation we use the keyword CHECK followed by a parenthesized condition to its CREATE TABLE statement.

To be a tuple based constraint, rather than an attribute based constraint (as in 10.2.2) the CHECK keyword must appear as a separate entry within the CREATE TABLE statement, so that it would not be associated with a specific attribute.

The condition in the "CHECK" constraint can be anything that could appear in a WHERE clause and will be evaluated whenever a tuple is to be inserted into the relation and/or whenever a tuple of the relation is updated.

The constraint condition might involve attributes in other relations, but the modification of values in these other relations will not trigger a re-evaluation of the constraint condition.

Constraints

Example:

```
CREATE TABLE Faculty(
    IDNumber CHAR(9) PRIMARY KEY,
    SocSecNum CHAR(9) UNIQUE,
    LastName VARCHAR(25),
    FirstName VARCHAR(25),
    Office CHAR(6) FOREIGN KEY
        REFERENCES Offices(OfficeID)
        ON DELETE SET NULL
        ON UPDATE CASCADE,
    Gender CHAR(1),
    CHECK ( (Gender='M' AND FirstName LIKE 'Mr.%')
    OR (Gender = 'F' AND FirstName LIKE 'Ms.%') )
);
```

10.2.4 Comparison of Tuple- and Attribute-Based Constraints

If a constraint on a tuple involves more than one attribute of that tuple then it must be written as a tuple based constraint, whereas if the constraint involves only one attribute of the tuple, then it is possible to write it either as a tuple- or an attribute based constraint.

When only one attribute of the tuple is involved, then the condition that gets checked will be the same, whether it is attribute or tuple-based, however, tuple based constraints will be checked more frequently than attribute based constraints, since tuple based constraints will be checked whenever the tuple is updated, but an attribute based constraint will be checked only when an update involves that attribute.

10.3 Modification of Constraints

It is possible to add, modify or delete constraints at any time. The way to make these changes depends on what kind of constraint it is, whether the constraint involved is associated with an attribute, a table or a database schema.

In order to modify or delete an existing constraint, it is necessary to identify the constraint, and to do this, it is necessary that the constraint have been assigned a name.

10.3.1 Giving Names to Constraints

To assign a name, we precede the constraint with the keyword CONSTRAINT and a name for the constraint.

Example:

```
CREATE TABLE Personnel(
    IDNumber CHAR(9) CONSTRAINT KeyID PRIMARY KEY,
    SocSecNum CHAR(9) CONSTRAINT UniqueSS UNIQUE,
    LastName VARCHAR(25),
    FirstName VARCHAR(25),
    Gender CHAR(1),
    CONSTRAINT RightTitle CHECK
        (
            (FirstName LIKE 'Dr.%') OR
            (Gender = 'M' AND FirstName LIKE 'Mr.%') OR
            (Gender = 'F' AND FirstName LIKE 'Ms.%')
        )
);
```

Constraints

10.3.2 Altering Constraints on Tables

We can change the checking of a constraint from immediate to deferred or deferred to immediate by means of the SET CONSTRAINT statement.

Example:

SET CONSTRAINT RightTitle DEFERRED;

Other changes to constraints can be modified using the ALTER TABLE statement.

The ALTER TABLE statement can be used to DROP existing constraints or to ADD new constraints.

Examples:

ALTER TABLE Faculty DROP CONSTRAINT RightTitle;

ALTER TABLE Faculty
    ADD CONSTRAINT NoAndro CHECK (Gender IN ('F', 'M'));

When we attempt to add a new constraint, the system will immediately check that all existing tuples in the relation satisfy the condition of the constraint. If any of the existing tuples fail to match the condition, the new constraint will be rejected.

10.4 Assertions

Assertions are part of the database schema, just as tables, and are among the most powerful forms of active elements in SQL.

An *assertion* is a boolean valued SQL expression that the system will require to be true at all times.

(Assertion checking can be deferred. In this case the checking will be done when/if the transaction is COMMIT'ed.)

The format for creating an assertion is:

CREATE ASSERTION <assertion-name> CHECK (<condition>)

where <condition> is essentially any condition that might appear in a WHERE clause.

The condition in an assertion must be true when the assertion is created and any database modification that will cause it to become false will be rejected, although, as just noted, it is possible to defer the checking of an assertion until a transaction commits (just as we can do with constraints.)

There is a distinct difference between the way CHECK constraints are written and the way *assertions* are written:

CHECK constraints are written as part of a specific relation, and can refer directly to attributes of that relation

Assertions are NOT defined as part of any specific relation. References to specific tuples/attributes require that they be identified (most commonly in a select-from-where expression.)

161

Constraints

Example:

```
CREATE ASSERTION ChairsHaveDoctorates CHECK
(
    NOT EXISTS
    (
        SELECT ChairID
        FROM DeptChairList, Personnel
        WHERE (ChairID=IDNumber) AND (FirstName NOT LIKE 'Dr.%')
    )
);
```

10.5 Chapter 10 Questions

10.5.1 True-False

10.5.1.1 If a relation R has a tuple based constraint, then its condition will be checked whenever a tuple in the relation is updated or a new tuple is added to the relation. The condition might also mention attributes in other relations. The condition will not be re-evaluated when one of these is modified.

10.5.1.2 If a constraint on a tuple involves more than one attribute of that tuple then it must be written as a tuple based constraint.

10.5.1.3 If a constraint on a tuple involves only one attribute of a tuple, then it must be written as a tuple based constraint.

10.5.1.4 Tuple based constraints will be checked more frequently than attribute based constraints.

10.5.1.5 If a constraint involves only one tuple in a relationship then it can be written as either a tuple based constraint or as an attribute based constraint.

10.5.1.6 Assertions are created using the CREATE ASSERTION statement.

10.5.1.7 It is possible to defer the checking of an assertion until a transaction commits.

10.5.2 Multiple Choice

10.5.2.1 If a relation R has a foreign key which references a relation S, then an attempt to modify a tuple in S in a way that results in a tuple in R having no reference in S, then: _____
a. The attempted modification of S will be rejected
b. The reference(s) in R will be changed to the new value for the tuple in S
c. Foreign key attribute(s) that reference the old value in S will be set to NULL
d. What happens will depend on the policy set by the programmer
e. none of the above

Constraints

10.5.2.2 If a relation R has a foreign key which references a relation S, the database designer might choose to deal with errors due to modifications of referenced attribute values in a tuple of S by _____

a. rejecting the modifications in S

b. copying the new values of attributes in S back into referencing tuples of R

c. setting to NULL all the foreign key attribute(s) of tuples in R which fail to reference any value in S

d. any of the above

e. none of the above

10.5.3 Completion

10.5.3.1 SQL supports a form of _____ integrity called foreign key constraint.

10.5.3.2 SQL allows us to specify that an attribute or a collection of attributes is a key for a relation by using the keywords PRIMARY KEY or the keyword _____.

10.5.3.3 One of the formats for declaring a foreign key is:

FOREIGN KEY (<attribute(s)>) _____ <table> (attribute(s)>)

10.5.3.4 Constraints can also be attached to attributes by the keyword _____ and a parenthesized condition that must hold for every value of that attribute

Views, Indexes and Privileges

11.0 Views and Indexes

Views (*Virtual Views*) are relations that are defined by queries. They are not stored in the database but can be queried just as if they were normal relations.

One particularly important (and very common) type of view is called an *index*.

11.1 Views

As we just said a (virtual) view is defined by a query. When a query references a virtual view the query processor will replace the view by its definition and compute the tuple values necessary to execute the query.

Views can also be constructed (periodically) from the database and the resulting relation stored, in order that they be accessed directly rather than recomputed.

Such a stored representation of the tuples produced by a view is called a *materialized* view.

Materialized views can be referenced as relations. Queries can simply read the tuples directly from the relation rather than have them (re)computed.

The existence of a materialized view can speed up the execution of queries, especially in the case of views that are accessed frequently.

An important example of a common type of materialized view is the *index*.

A specialized type of stored data structure designed to speed up access to specified tuples of one of the stored relations.

A *normal* relation (a relation that is defined with a CREATE TABLE statement) will actually exist as part of the database. The SQL system stores these tables in some physical organization. Such relations are *persistent*.

They can be expected to exist indefinitely and it is expected that they will not to change unless told to do so by an SQL modification statement.

Views (virtual views), however, form a class of SQL relations that do NOT (necessarily) exist physically.

Even materialized views do not generally exist during the time periods between sessions (i.e. are *not persistent*.)

Views are defined by expressions (much like queries) but can be queried as if they existed physically.

164

Views, Indexes and Privileges

11.1.1 Declaring Views

The simplest form of view definition is:

    CREATE VIEW <view name> AS <view definition>

where <view definition> is an SQL query •

Example1:

    CREATE VIEW PhoneBook AS
        SELECT LastName, FirstName, OfficeID, OfficePhone
        FROM Personnel NATURAL JOIN (Faculty NATURAL JOIN Offices);

Example2:

    CREATE VIEW ClassRosters AS
        SELECT IDNumber, ProgramID, CourseNumber, SectionNumber, Credits
        FROM Classes NATURAL JOIN EnrolledIn
        ORDER BY ProgramID, CourseNumber, SectionNumber;

11.1.2 Querying Views

A view can be queried, exactly as if it were a standard table. We can use its name in a FROM clause and the DBMS will produce the described tuples by operating on the relations used to define the view.

Example:

    SELECT IDNumber, SUM(Credits)
    FROM ClassRosters
    GROUP BY IDNumber;

11.1.3 Renaming Attributes

Sometimes we might want to give a view's attributes names of our own choosing, rather than those that come out of the query defining the view. We can do this by surrounding the new attribute names with parentheses following the view's name in the creation command.

Example:

    CREATE VIEW PhoneBook(Lst, First, Phone) AS
        SELECT LastName, FirstName, OfficePhone
        FROM Personnel NATURAL JOIN (Faculty NATURAL JOIN Offices);

11.2 ModifyingViews

In a few situations it might be desirable to execute an insertion, deletion or update to a view. It is possible to perform a few of these actions in some (limited) circumstances.

Views, Indexes and Privileges

11.2.1 Removing a View

The most extreme modification of a view, and at the same time the simplest, is to delete it altogether. Since a view does not exist as a collection of tuples, but rather as a query, deleting it will have no effect on any underlying base tables.

The command to delete a view is:

DROP VIEW <name of view>

Unlike other view modifications, DROP VIEW can be performed on any view.

Insertions and updates, on the other hand, do involve modifications of underlying base tables, and cannot be only be performed on all views, only on a limited class of views, known as updatable views.

11.2.2 Updatable Views

SQL provides a formal definition of which views support insertion and/or update (actions that will involve modifications of underlying tables.) This definition, however, is quite complex.

The following is a simplified version of the rules:

A view is said to be *updatable* if, in its defining query:

The FROM clause has the form
FROM R
where R is a single table.

The list of attributes in the SELECT clause includes the primary key from the table R

The SELECT clause does not include the DISTINCT restriction.

Any attribute of the table R not included in the SELECT list has a default value or permits the NULL value.

The WHERE clause does not include R in a subquery.

Under these conditions:

Each tuple produced by the defining query will be associated with a unique tuple in R.

Any modification carried out on a value of the view can be translated back to a value in R.

Assuming our "Classes" relation had been created by the following command:

```
CREATE TABLE Classes(
    ProgramID: CHAR(4),
    CourseNumber:INT,
    SectionNumber:INT,
    TeacherIDNumber: CHAR(9)
        FOREIGN KEY REFERENCES Faculty (IDNumber),
    RoomID:CHAR(6)
        FOREIGN KEY REFERENCES Classroom (RoomID),
    PRIMARY KEY (ProgramID, CourseNumber, SectionNumber)
);
```

With the above definition, the attributes "TeacherIDNumber" and "RoomID" would default to NULL.

The early dbms transactions involving classes might be processed relatively simply (and more efficiently) using a view like the following:

```
CREATE VIEW SimpleClass(Prg, Crs, Sec) AS
    SELECT ProgramID, CourseNumber, SectionNumber
    FROM Classes;
```

The view "SimpleClass" IS updateable and can be used for the most common actions involving classes, actions such as enrolling a student in the class, deleting a student from the class, creating a list of students enrolled in the class.

Working with this view avoids the complication of dealing with unnecessary teacher and classroom information:

Since the "SimpleClass" view is updateable, the following command is also legal:

```
INSERT INTO SimpleClass(Prg, Crs, Sec)
VALUES ('COMP', '3004', '021')
```

This command adds a new tuple to the "Classes" relation. This new tuple will have attribute attributes:

('COMP', '3004','021', NULL, NULL)

11.3 Materialized Views

A view describes how a new relation can be constructed from existing tables in the database by executing a query on the tables.

If a view is used frequently enough, it may be efficient to *materialize* it, i.e. to maintain its value(s) as a relation in memory rather than recompute it/them every time needed. There is, of course, a *cost* to maintaining such a materialized view. In addition to the storage space it occupies, it also increases the complexity (and time required) for modification of underlying tables. Each time such a modification takes place, the materialized view must also be recomputed (at least *in principle* the view should be recomputed.)

In principle, the DBMS should recompute a materialized view each time one of its base tables changes in any way. For *some* views, however, it is possible to limit the number the number of changes of the view and/or to limit the amount of work in maintaining the view.

Clearly if the "SimpleClass" view defined above in 11.2.2 was materialized, changes in values of the "Classes" attributes "TeacherIDNumber" and/or "RoomID would not require updating the view, since these values do not appear in the tuples that comprise the view.

Another (rather common) setting in which materialized views can be used to good effect is one in which the view would only be needed/used on predictable occasions at reasonably long periods of time. Such a view could be updated periodically at times of low utilization (possibly nighttimes and/or on weekends.)

Views, Indexes and Privileges

11.4 Indexes in SQL

An *index* for a relation is a specific kind of data structure that improves the efficiency of certain kinds of database searches.

We can understand indexes by thinking of them as binary search trees of (*keyvalue*, *resulttuple*) pairs where each *keyvalue* is associated with *resulttuple*, a location where a set of associated result values is located.

Such an index can improve the efficiency of many kinds of searches involving the searched attribute and especially those in which attribute value is compared with a constant.

11.4.1 Motivation for using Indexes

When relations are very large, it becomes expensive to scan all tuples of a relation to find the (possibly very few) tuples that match a condition.

If, for example, our example college were to have 10,000 students then a query like

SELECT IDNumber
FROM Personnel
WHERE LastName='Latrans';

would require more than 10,000 read and scan operations, but if the relation "Personnel" were to have an index on attribute "LastName", then the student(s)/professors having 'Latrans' as "LastName" value(s) could be located with fewer than 15 operations.

Indexes can be especially useful in queries that involve a join. Again, assuming that our college has 10,000 students it is not unreasonable that relation EnrolledIn would have between 30,000 and 40,000 tuples. With no indexes to simplify the searches, executing the query

SELECT ProgramID, CourseNumber, SectionNumber
FROM (Personnel NATURAL JOIN Students) NATURAL JOIN EnrolledIN
WHERE LastName='Lugo' and FirstName='Belinda';

will first require 10,000 operations to identify the "IDNumber" values for all students named Belinda Lugo, and then another 30,000+ operations to identify all EnrolledIn tuples having those "IDNumber" values. If, on the other hand, we were to have a "Student" index based on attribute "LastName" and an "EnrolledIn" index based on IDNumber, then it would require less than 20 operations to identify the "IDNumber" values of students named Belinda Lugo (it is likely that there is only one such student) and then, if we have with an "EnrolledIn" index based on attribute "IDNumber", it would require less than 20 operations to identify all "EnrolledIn" tuples having that "IDNumber" value.

11.4.2 Declaring Indexes

In fact, indexes are not part of the SQL standard (at least up through SQL-99.) Most commercial systems, however, (probably all of them) have included a way for designers to specify indexes[18].

The following example would illustrate a typical format:

CREATE INDEX IDIndex ON EnrolledIn(IDNumber);

After this declaration, any query specifying an EnrolledIn IDNumber can be executed in a way that examines only EnrolledIn tuples having that IDNumber value. This should result in a significant decrease in time to execute the query.

Often (almost always) a DBMS will allow us to specify an index on multiple attributes. These would be binary search trees of (*key*, *value*) pairs where *key* is a *combination* of values from the multiple attributes and *value* is the set of tuples with that combination of values for the attributes.

11.4.3 To Index or not to Index

Although indexes improve the time required to execute many queries, they do not come without costs.

Indexes require storage space. If storage is likely to be limited, then the designer must pick and choose, limiting the indexes to only those most useful.

As mentioned above, there is no official standard for indexes in SQL. This means that, although all DBMS systems support indexes, there is no guarantee that they do so uniformly. If a database includes indexes, then they could conceivably create portability problems.

The existence of an index on an attribute can greatly speed up the execution of queries in which a value or range of values is specified for that attribute, and, as we noted, the speedup can be particularly dramatic for queries that specify a join on the attribute. On the other hand, as with materialized views[19], having an index on an attribute for a relation makes insertions, deletions and updates of that relation much more complex and time consuming. In systems where updates will be frequent (and data queries relatively infrequent) the designer should try to avoid introducing many indexes.

11.4.3 Selection of Indexes

The choice of what indexes to include is one of the principal factors that will influence the performance of a database.

11.4.3.1 Primary Key as Index

Often the most useful index for a relation is its key.

In fact, many DBMS systems automatically index the primary key for each relation.

There are two reasons that primary key indexes are useful:

Queries that specify the key are common, so indexes on the primary keys would be likely to be used frequently.

Since there is only one tuple with a given value for a key, a search can terminate immediately upon finding that tuple.

---

[18] Certainly all of the *successful* commercial systems have included indexes.
[19] An index is, in fact, a type of materialized view.

11.4.3.2 Other Useful Indexes

We can also identify two situations where a nonkey index can be particularly effective:

If an attribute is *almost* a key

If very few tuples would have any given value for that attribute, then queries referencing a value for that attribute would require relatively few disk accesses to find all of the tuples

If tuple storage is clustered on the attribute

Most (preferably all) of the tuples with a given value would be in the same section (block/page) of the disk.

Reading this block into RAM to access one of the tuples would bring all (or at least most) of the others into RAM as well. These, then, could be accessed relatively quickly (RAM access is, after all, MUCH faster than disk access.)

11.5 Security in SQL

Most databases are accessed by multiple users (frequently simultaneously) but, as a general rule, not all users will have the same rights and privileges. Some of the users will be allowed to access some data and others will be allowed access to other data. Some users will be allowed to modify data while others will only be allowed to read the data.

Clearly, then, a DBMS must have some system for identifying users, tracking their rights and privileges and enforcing restrictions. The possibility always exists that a user might attempt some activity for which he does *not* hold the right or privilege. The system must recognize when that happens and take appropriate actions.

SQL is designed to support the division of users into distinct classes and to assign different rights and privileges for different kinds of database activities to the different classes. These rights and privileges are assigned using the GRANT instruction (and are *de*-assigned using the REVOKE instruction.)

When an object (table, view, function, procedure …) is created, the user who creates the object (the *owner* of the object) has full privileges on the object. No other users have privileges on the object until the owner grants privileges to them.

11.5.1 Authorization ID's

SQL postulates the existence of what it calls *Authorization ID's*.

These are, essentially, what most of us would call *usernames* and groups of users/usernames that the system administrator chooses to create.

The SQL standard requires the existence of a specific Authorization ID called *PUBLIC* which will include *all* users.

SQL supports the assignment of privileges to Authorization ID's (much as privileges such as the read, write and execute privileges are assigned by a file system management system.)

Since databases are more complex than file systems, the system of privileges used in SQL is more complex that of most file systems.

11.5.2 Privileges

The GRANT statement is used to grant specific privileges to users or to roles, or to grant roles to users or to roles. The REVOKE statement is used to revoke privileges and role grants.

Among the grant and revoke privileges are:

- SELECT

- INSERT

- DELETE

- UPDATE

- REFERENCES

- TRIGGER

The first four of these privileges (SELECT, INSERT, DELETE, and UPDATE) apply to relations (tables or views.) They give the holder of the privilege the right (as the names would imply) to query the relation, to insert tuples into the relation, to delete tuples from the relation and to modify values in the relation.

The SELECT, INSERT and UPDATE statements may also involve a list of attributes. If there is such an attribute list, then the holder will only be allowed to reference/modify those attributes.

The REFERENCES privilege is the right to reference a relation in an integrity constraint. The REFERENCES privilege might also include an attached list of attributes, in which case the holder would only be allowed to reference those attributes in the integrity constraints.

The TRIGGER privilege on a relation is the right to define triggers on that relation.

11.5.3 Granting Privileges

The owner/creator of a relation will have all of privileges for that relation. He/she may give privileges for the relation to another user/authorization ID or group (list) of users by executing the GRANT statement.

```
GRANT <privilege list> ON <database element> TO <user list>
    [WITH GRANT OPTION]
```

If the GRANT statement includes the "WITH GRANT OPTION" option, then any user in the "user-list" can, in turn, grant the privilege(s) that he/she has been assigned to other users.

Views, Indexes and Privileges

Let us assume that, in our example college, *sowling* is the Authorization ID of the chairman of the MATH and that *hlechapeau* is that of the registrar.

The database administrator might create a view:

    CREATE VIEW MathEnroll AS
        SELECT *
        FROM EnrolledIn
        WHERE ProgramID='MATH';

Then it would be reasonable to assign privileges:
    GRANT SELECT, INSERT, DELETE, UPDATE
    ON MathEnroll
    TO sowling, hlechapeau
    WITH GRANT OPTION;

Since this assignment includes the GRANT option, Dr. Owling could execute the following , in order that his secretary would have some access:
    GRANT SELECT(CourseNumber, SectionNumber), UPDATE(SectionNumber)
    ON MathEnroll
    TO plasilla;

This GRANT instruction does *not* include "WITH GRANT OPTION" and so plasilla cannot give access to other users.

11.5.4 Revoking Privileges

A user who has GRANT'ed a privilege to another user can later REVOKE that privilege or dependent privileges (i.e the owner of MathEnroll can revoke Owlings UPDATE privilege for just the dependent attributes "ProgramID", "IDNumber" and "EnrollmentTypeID", and allow him to update the remaining attributes.)

The form of the REVOKE instruction is:

    REVOKE <privilege list> ON <database element> FROM <user list>
        (CASCADE | RESTRICT)

It is conceivable that a user who has been GRANT'ed a privilege might have GRANT'ed that privilege to another user (as sowling has GRANT'ed certain privileges to plasilla.) Clearly a user cannot be allowed to GRANT privileges he/she does not have, so the system must determine what to do in this case, and that is what the keywords CASCADE and RESTRICT control.

If the REVOKE instruction ends with RESTRICT and if any revoked privilege has been GRANT'ed by any user in the user list, then the REVOKE instruction cannot be executed.

If the REVOKE instruction ends with CASCADE then the REVOKE statement will be executed and any of the REVOKed privileges that had been GRANTed by any of the affected users will also be revoked.

Views, Indexes and Privileges

If the owner of MathEnroll were to attempt to execute:

    REVOKE UPDATE ON MathEnroll FROM sowling RESTRICT;

the instruction would fail to execute since the GRANT by sowling depended on his having privilege UPDATE.

If, on the other hand the instruction had been:

    REVOKE UPDATE ON MathEnroll FROM sowling CASCADE;

then the instruction would execute, sowling would lose his UPDATE privilege and plasilla would also lose her update privilege (limited though it may have been.)

The granting of privileges by users can result in complex interrelationships of privileges and unexpected consequences of REVOKE ... CASCADE executions.

Views, Indexes and Privileges

11.6 Chapter 11 Questions

  11.6.1 True-False

    11.6.1.1 A view can only be queried to produce the value(s) of a single attribute.

    11.6.1.2 We can give a view's attributes names of our own choosing, by surrounding the new attribute names with parentheses following the view's name in the creation command.

    11.6.1.3 In limited circumstances, it is possible to execute insertions, deletions or updates on a view.

    11.6.1.4 The DROP VIEW command can only be performed on updatable views.

    11.6.1.5 Each time one of the underlying tables of a materialized view is modified, the view must be recomputed.

    11.6.1.6 Indexes are not part of any SQL standard (at least up through SQL-99)

    11.6.1.7 Because indexes are not part of any SQL standard, they are included in very few commercial systems.

    11.6.1.8 Most DBMS will allow us to specify an index on multiple attributes

    11.6.1.9 Most databases are accessed by multiple users, frequently simultaneously. Not all users will have the same rights and privileges.

    11.6.1.10 When an object (table, view, function, procedure …) is created, the user who creates the object (the *owner* of the object) has full privileges on the object. No other users have privileges on the object until the owner grants privileges to them.

    11.6.1.11 Since databases are more complex than file systems, the kinds of privileges used in SQL are more complex that are those of file systems.

    11.6.1.12 The privileges SELECT, INSERT, DELETE and UPDATE may involve a list of attributes, in which case the holder is only allowed to reference/modify those attributes.

    11.6.1.13 The owner/creator of a relation will have all of privileges for that relation. He/she may give privileges for the relation to another user/authorization ID or group (list) of users by executing the GRANT statement.

    11.6.1.14 The form of the REVOKE instruction is:

      REVOKE <privilege list> ON <database element-list> FROM <user list>
      (CASCADE | RESTRICT)

  11.6.2 Multiple Choice

    11.6.2.1 Virtual views
      a. are stored in the database, and can be queried
      b. are not stored in the database, but can be queried
      c. are stored in the database, but cannot be queried
      d. are not stored in the database, and cannot be queried
      e. none of the above

11.6.2.2 The command to delete a view is:

          _____ VIEW *<name of view>*
   a. DROP
   b. DELETE
   c. ERASE
   d. KILL
   e. none of the above

11.6.2.3 A disadvantage of adding indexes to a database is _____
   a. indexes use storage space
   b. databases with indexes might have problems of portability
   c. updating databases with indexes can be complex ant time consuming
   d. all of the above
   e. none of the above

11.6.2.4 The _____ privilege is the right to use a relation in an integrity constraint.
   a. REFERENCES
   b. ACCESS
   c. INTEGRITY
   d. all of the above
   e. none of the above

11.6.3 Completion

11.6.3.1 *Virtual* views are _____ that are defined by queries over other relations.

11.6.3.2 A view is defined by a(n) _____

11.6.3.3 If a view is used frequently enough, it may be efficient to _____ it
   – To maintain its value at all times.

11.6.3.4 Rights and privileges are assigned using the GRANT instruction (and de-assigned using the _____ instruction.)

11.6.3.5 If the REVOKE instruction ends with the _____ keyword and if any revoked privilege has been GRANT'ed by any user in the user list, then the REVOKE instruction cannot be executed

Answers to Odd Numbered Questions

Answers to Odd Numbered Questions

1.11 Chapter 1 Questions

1.11.1 TRUE/FALSE

1.11.1.1 In common parlance, the term database tends to refer to a collection of data that is managed by a DBMS

Ans: T

1.11.1.3 Early DBMS's did not support high level query languages.

Ans: T

1.11.2 MULTIPLE CHOICE

1.11.2.1 A DBMS will typically be controlled by commands (and programs) written in _____, a language originally designed by IBM but which has since been adopted (with minor variations) by all designers of DBMS software.

- **A.** **SQL**
- b. ISO
- c. ANSI
- d. Oracle
- e. none of the above

1.11.2.3 The data in a database will normally be:
- a. *integrated* but not *shared*
- b. *shared* but not *integrated*
- **C.** **both *integrated* and *shared***
- d. neither *integrated* nor *shared*
- e. none of the above

1.11.3 COMPLETION

1.11.3.1 A(n) _____ system is a computerized record-keeping system – A system whose purpose is to store information and allow users to update and retrieve the information

Ans: database

1.11.3.3 There were several early DBMS models used for describing the structure of database information. Prominent among them:
- The _____ (tree based) model
- The graph based (network) model

Ans: hierarchical

1.11.3.5 By the 1990's the _____ model had become the norm

Ans: relational

1.11.3.7 When we say that the data in a database is _____ we mean that the data will be stored in several distinct files, but that most redundancies will have been eliminated

Ans: integrated

2.11 Chapter 2 Questions:

2.11.1 TRUE/FALSE

2.11.1.1 Semistructured models are more flexible than relational models

Ans: T

2.11.1.3 The *relational* model is more widely used in DBMS's than semistructured models

Ans: T

2.11.1.5 The type CHAR(n) declares a fixed length string of n characters

Ans: T

2.11.2 MULTIPLE CHOICE

2.11.2.1 An important concept involved in data models is
a. Structure of data
b. Operations on data
c. Constraints on data
D. all of the above
e. none of the above

2.11.3 COMPLETION

2.11.3.1 The notion of a data _____ is fundamental to the study of database systems

Ans: model

2.11.3.3 In a database data model, operations that retrieve information are referred to as _____

Ans: queries

2.11.3.5 The relational database model is based on _____

Ans: tables

2.11.3.7 A modern trend is to add _____ oriented features to the relational model

Ans: object

2.11.3.9 We use the term "_____" to describe the *meanings* of the entries in the columns

Ans: attributes

2.11.3.11 The relational model requires that each entry in each tuple be _____

Ans: atomic

2.11.3.13 _____ is the principal language used to describe and manipulate relational databases

Ans: SQL

2.11.3.15 SQL makes a distinction between three kinds of relations:
- Stored relations (tables)
  - The most common kind of relation
  - A relation that exists in the database, can be modified (by changing its tuples) and can be queried
  - The CREATE TABLE statement declares a schema for a stored relation
    - Assigns names for table and attributes. Specifies data types for attributes. Specifies keys.

- _____
  - Relations defined by computation
  - Not stored, but constructed (in whole or in part) when needed
- Temporary tables
  - Constructed by the SQL processor while executing queries and data modifications
    - These relations are thrown away, not stored

  Ans: views

3.4 Chapter 3 Questions:

3.4.1 True-False

3.4.1.1 Relational Algebra (like all algebras) allows us to form expressions of arbitrary complexity, by applying operations to results of other operations

Ans: T

3.4.2 Multiple Choice

3.4.2.1 $R \cup S$, the *union* of R and S, is
  A. the collection of elements that are in R, in S, or in both.
  b. the collection of all elements that are in *both* R *and* S
  c. the collection of elements that are in R but not in S
  d. the collection of elements that are in S but not in R
  e. none of the above

3.2.2.3 $R \bowtie_C S$ represents the _____ join of R and S

  a. C
  B. theta
  c. natural
  d. complete
  e. none of the above

3.4.3 Completion

3.4.3.1 In a database model, there must be operations to query and modify the data. At the base of querying and modifying data is a _____ *algebra*
ANS: relational
3.4.3.3 We generally refer to expressions of relational algebra as _____
ANS: queries
3.4.3.5 _____ place limitations/restrictions on the data that may be stored in a database
ANS: Constraints

Answers to Odd Numbered Questions

4.4 Chapter 4 Questions:

4.4.1 True-False

4.4.1.1 It is common for an initial relational schema to have room for improvement.

Ans: T

4.4.1.3 Most relations do not have superkeys.

Ans: F Every relation has at least one superkey: The collection of ALL attributes.

4.4.1.5 The splitting/combining rule says we may *split* an FD of the form
$A_1, A_2, ..., A_n \rightarrow B_1, B_2, ..., B_m$
into several simpler FD's (having only one attribute on the right hand side.)

Ans: T

4.4.1.7 *redundancy* is an inefficient use of storage, but, much worse, it introduces the potential for several kinds of errors.

Ans: T

4.4.2 Multiple Choice

4.4.2.1 A principal kind of anomaly that we encounter in database design is:

   a.   redundancy
   b.   update anomaly
   c.   deletion anomaly
   D   all of the above
   e.   none of the above

4.4.3 Completion

4.4.3.1 It is common for an initial relational schema to have room for improvement
   – Especially by removing _____
Ans: redundancies
4.4.3.3 A constraint C on a relation R is said to be _____ if every instance of R satisfies C.
Ans: trivial
4.4.3.5 Lack of care in the design of a database can lead to redundancy and _____.

Ans: anomalies

5.6 Chapter 5 Questions

5.6.1 True-False

5.6.1.1 The goal of decomposition is to replace a single relation with several that have no anomalies.

Ans: T

5.6.1.3 If a relation is decomposed according to the algorithm described in Section 5.1.3.1 of this text, all of the information can be recovered faithfully by the natural join.

Ans: T

5.6.1.5 If $\{B_1,\ldots,B_m\}$ is contained in $\{A_1,\ldots,A_n\}$ then $A_1,\ldots,A_n \rightarrow B_1,\ldots,B_m$.

Ans: T

5.6.1.7 BCNF implies 4NF.

Ans: F 4NF implies BCNF

5.6.1.9 The major difference between FD's and MVD's, from the point of view of the chase, is that, while an MVD tends to show us that (existing) entries in a given column, must be equal, an FD will imply that there must be another tuple in the relation, having component values those of existing tuples, but swapped.

Ans: T

5.6.2 Multiple Choice

5.6.2.1 If it is possible to obtain all of the information in a relation from a decomposition, then the decomposition is called a _____
   A   lossless join
   b.   faithful join
   c.   lossless projection
   d.   faithful projection
   e.   none of the above

5.6.3 Completion

5.6.3.1 A relation R is in _____ if, the left side of every nontrivial FD contains a key.

Ans: BCNF

5.6.3.3 An attribute that is a member of some key is sometimes said to be _____.

Ans: prime

6.7 Chapter 6 Questions

6.7.1 True-False

6.7.1.1 Although almost all commercial database managers use the relational model, it is usually easier to start with a higher level model and then convert to a relational model.

Ans: T

6.7.1.3 Attributes tend to be easier to implement than entity sets and/or relationships, but too many attributes can cause problems.

Ans: T

6.7.1.5 When converting from E/R diagram to relational design, a supporting relationship from a weak entity set to a supporting entity set need not be converted to a relation.

Ans: T

Answers to Odd Numbered Questions

6.7.2 Multiple Choice

6.7.2.1 Which of the following models can represent multiway relationships
   a. E/R
   b. UML
   c. ODL
   D. all of the above
   e. none of the above

6.7.2.3 In converting an E/R representation of an isa-hierarchy, there are several strategies that might be used. One is: For each possible subtree (that includes the root) create a relation whose schema include all attributes of entity sets in the subtree.
   This strategy is called
   a. Follow the E/R viewpoint
   B. Treat entities as objects belonging to a single class
   c. Use null values
   d. any of the above
   e. none of the above

6.7.3 Completion

6.7.3.1 In the *entity-relationship model* (E/R model) the structure of data is represented graphically as an E/R diagram using three principal element types:
   – _____ sets
   – Attributes
   – Relationships

Ans:_Entity_

6.7.3.3 _____ are *connections* between entity sets

Ans: Relationships

6.7.3.5 We connect an entity set to a subclass with a special kind of relationship called a(n)_____

Ans: isa

6.7.3.7 A referential-_____ constraint says that a value appearing in one context must also appear in another.

Ans: integrity

6.7.3.9 If E is a weak entity set, then its key must consist of:
   – Zero or more of its own attributes
   – One or more key attributes that are reached by many-one relationships
   • These many-one relationships are called _____ *relationships*

Ans: supporting

7.8 Chapter 7 Questions

7.8.1 True-False

7.8.1.1 UML (Unified Modeling Language) was originally developed as a graphical notation for describing database designs. It has been extended (with some modifications) to a notation for describing software designs in an object oriented style.

Ans: F UML (Unified Modeling Language) was originally developed as a graphical notation for describing software designs in an object oriented style. It has been extended (with some modifications) to a notation for describing database designs

7.8.1.3 The meaning of an open diamond in an aggregation is similar to a 0..1 constraint.

Ans: T

7.8.1.5 In a UML system it is possible that we might have more information than in an E/R system.

Ans: T

7.8.1.7 The declaration of keys for a class is optional in ODL

Ans T

7.8.2 Multiple Choice

7.8.2.1 The UML term for what in an E/R diagram would be called a binary relationship is:
a. class
B. association
c. subclass
d. any of the above
e. none of the above

7.8.2.3 In a UML diagram, a line between two classes that has a solid diamond at one end represents a(n)
a. association
b. binding
c. aggregation
D. composition
e. none of the above

7.8.2.5 If we have a _____ relationship from C to D, then the type of relation in C is just D while that in D is Set<C>
a. many-many
B. many-one
c. one-one
d. any of the above
e. none of the above

7.8.3 Completion

7.8.3.1 A(n) ___ in UML is similar to an entity set in the E/R model.

Ans: class

7.8.3.3 UML permits a class C to have any of four different kinds of subclasses:
    –Subclasses of C can be complete or partial.
    –Subclasses of C can be disjoint or _____

Ans: overlapping

7.8.3.5 ODL offers the database designer a system for constructing _____ types that is similar to that found in many modern languages.

8.3 Chapter 8 Questions

8.3.1 True-False

8.3.1.1 Sets generally reflect the way the relational model is implemented in practice better than do bags.

Ans F Bags generally reflect the way the relational model is implemented in practice better than sets.

8.3.1.3 Commercial DBMS's implement relations as sets rather than bags.

Ans: F Commercial DBMS's implement relations as bags rather than sets.

8.3.1.5 Unions, intersections and differences have slightly different definitions for bags than they do for sets.

Ans T

8.3.2 Multiple Choice

8.3.2.1 The bag union $R \cup S$ is a bag in which (5,6) appears _____ times

A	B
1	2
3	4
1	2
1	2
R	

A	B
1	2
3	4
3	4
5	6
S	

A. 1
b. 2
c. 3
d. 4
e. none of the above

8.3.2.3 The *duplicate-elimination* operator _____ turns a bag into a set by eliminating all but one copy of each tuple.
   A. δ
   b. τ
   c. g
   d. σ
   e. none of the above

8.3.2.5 The *sorting* operator _____ turns a relation into a list of tuples sorted according to one or more attributes.
   a. δ
   B. τ
   c. g
   d. σ
   e. none of the above

8.3.3 Completion

8.3.3.1 In this chapter we will extend the set based algebra to _____.

   –   This better reflects the way the relational model is implemented in practice
Ans: bags

8.3.3.3 The standard aggregate operators are:
   • _____ produces the sum of the entries in a column with numerical values
   • AVG produces the average of the entries in a column with numerical values
   • MIN and MAX produces the smallest/largest value in a column with entries that can be compared in "size" or order
   • COUNT produces the number of (not necessarily distinct) entries in a column

Ans SUM

9.14 Chapter 9 Questions

9.14.1 True-False

9.14.1.1 There are many different dialects of SQL

Ans: T

9.14.1.3 Strings in SQL are denoted by surrounding them by either single quotes or double quotes.

Ans: F Strings in SQL are denoted by surrounding them by single quotes

9.14.1.5 Strings in SQL can be stored as either fixed length sequences or as variable length sequences.

Ans: T

9.14.1.7 The query:

SELECT * FROM *Courses NATURAL LEFT OUTER JOIN Classes;*

produces a relation in which every tuple from relation Classes appears in at least one tuple. If the tuple does not match any tuple from Courses, then the Courses attributes that do not appear in Classes will have null values.

Ans: F The query:

SELECT * FROM *Courses NATURAL LEFT OUTER JOIN Classes;*

produces a relation in which every tuple from relation Courses appears in at least one tuple. If the tuple does not match any tuple from Classes, then the Classes attributes that do not appear in Courses will have null values.

9.14.2 Multiple Choice

9.14.2.1 Most *SQL queries use the keyword* _____
  a. SELECT
  b. FROM
  c. WHERE
  D. all of the above
  e. none of the above

9.14.2.3 The operator _____ normally eliminates duplicates
  a. UNION
  b. INTERSECT
  c. EXCEPT
  D. all of the above
  e. none of the above

9.14.3 Completion

9.14.3.1 The most commonly used relational DBMS's use a language called _____ to query and modify the databases.

Ans: SQL

9.14.3.3 In an SQL query, the _____ clause is a condition. Tuples must satisfy this condition in order to match the query and be part of the query result.

Ans: WHERE

9.14.3.5 Sometimes we wish to produce a relation with column headers different from the attribute names from the original relation.
  • We can achieve this effect using the keyword _____ following the original name of the attribute

Ans: AS

9.14.3.7 SQL provides the capability to compare strings on the basis of simple pattern matching.
  – Using the form :
     s LIKE p
  where s is a string and p is a *pattern*
  • Ordinary characters in p match the same characters in s.
    The character _____ matches any sequence of 0 or more characters in s

Ans: %

9.14.3.9 We can assign a (n) _____ (also known as a *tuple variable*) to any relation in the FROM statement

Ans: alias

9.14.3.11 A value that can appear as one component of a tuple is referred to as a(n) _____

Ans: scalar

9.14.3.13 _____ R is a condition that will be true if and only if R is nonempty.

Ans: EXISTS

9.14.3.15 To change the value of an attribute in a tuple that already exists, we use the SQL _____ operator.

Ans: UPDATE

9.14.3.17 The SQL statement _____ causes the transaction to end successfully. Changes made since transaction began are installed permanently to database.

Ans: COMMIT

10.5 Chapter 10 Questions

10.5.1 True-False

10.5.1.1 If a relation R has a tuple based constraint, then its condition will be checked whenever a tuple in the relation is updated or a new tuple is added to the relation. The condition might also mention attributes in other relations. The condition will not be re-evaluated when one of these is modified.

Ans T

10.5.1.3 If a constraint on a tuple involves only one attribute of a tuple, then it must be written as a tuple based constraint.

Ans: F If a constraint on a tuple involves only one attribute of a tuple, then it can be written either as a tuple- or an attribute-based constraint

10.5.1.5 If a constraint involves only one tuple in a relationship then it can be written as either a tuple based constraint or as an attribute based constraint.

Ans: F If a constraint involving a tuple involves more than one *attribute* of that tuple then it *must* be written as a tuple based constraint

Answers to Odd Numbered Questions

10.5.1.7 It is possible to defer the checking of an assertion until a transaction commits.

Ans: T

10.5.2 Multiple Choice

10.5.2.1 If a relation R has a foreign key which references a relation S, then an attempt to modify a tuple in S in a way that results in a tuple in R having no reference in S, then: _____

  a. The attempted modification of S will be rejected
  b. The reference(s) in R will be changed to the new value for the tuple in S
  c. Foreign key attribute(s) that reference the old value in S will be set to NULL
  D. What happens will depend on the policy set by the programmer
  e. none of the above.

10.5.3 Completion

10.5.3.1 SQL supports a form of _____ integrity called foreign key constraint.

Ans: referential

10.5.3.3 One of the formats for declaring a foreign key is:
    FOREIGN KEY (<attribute(s)>) _____ <table> (attribute(s)>)
Ans: REFERENCES

11.6 Chapter 11 Questions

11.6.1 True-False

11.6.1.1 A view can only be queried to produce the value(s) of a single attribute.

Ans: F A view may be queried, exactly as if it were a standard table.

11.6.1.3 In limited circumstances, it is possible to execute insertions, deletions or updates on a view.

Ans: T

11.6.1.5 Each time one of the underlying tables of a materialized view is modified, the view must be recomputed.

Ans: F Although in principle, the DBMS should recompute a materialized view each time one of its base tables changes in any way, for some views, it is possible to limit the number the number of changes of the view and/or to limit the amount of work in maintaining the view.

11.6.1.7 Because indexes are not part of any SQL standard, they are included in very few commercial systems.

Ans: F Most commercial DBMS systems have included a way for designers to specify indexes.

11.6.1.9 Most databases are accessed by multiple users, frequently simultaneously. Not all users will have the same rights and privileges.

Ans: T

11.6.1.11 Since databases are more complex than file systems, the kinds of privileges used in SQL are more complex that are those of file systems.

Ans: T

11.6.1.13 The owner/creator of a relation will have all of privileges for that relation. He/she may give privileges for the relation to another user/authorization ID or group (list) of users by executing the GRANT statement.

Ans: T

11.6.2 Multiple Choice

11.6.2.1 Virtual views
   A. are stored in the database, and can be queried
   b. are not stored in the database, but can be queried
   c. are stored in the database, but cannot be queried
   d. are not stored in the database, and cannot be queried
   e. none of the above

11.6.2.3 A disadvantage of adding indexes to a database is _____
   a. indexes use storage space
   b. databases with indexes might have problems of portability
   c. updating databases with indexes can be complex ant time consuming
   D. all of the above
   e. none of the above

11.6.3 Completion

11.6.3.1 *Virtual* views are _____ that are defined by queries over other relations.

Ans: relations

11.6.3.3 If a view is used frequently enough, it may be efficient to _____ it
   – To maintain its value at all times

Ans: materialize

11.6.3.5 If the REVOKE instruction ends with the _____ keyword and if any revoked privilege has been GRANT'ed by any user in the user list, then the REVOKE instruction cannot be executed

Ans: RESTRICT

---

[i] A First Course in Database Systems, by Ullman and Widom, Pearson/Prentice-Hall

www.ingramcontent.com/pod-product-compliance
Lightning Source LLC
LaVergne TN
LVHW081342050326
832903LV00024B/1262